Survival Guns:
A Beginner's Guide

By

Steve Markwith

Part of the PrepSmart series of books published by:

Dystopian Fiction & Survival Nonfiction

Go to **PrepperPress.com/PrepSmart**
for other books in the PrepSmart series.

Survival Guns: A Beginner's Guide

ISBN 978-0692236673

Printed in the United States of America.

Prepper Press Trade Paperback Edition: July 2014

Prepper Press is a division of Kennebec Publishing, LLC

About the Author

Steve Markwtih holds a lifelong interest in all things that shoot. This includes rifles, shotguns, revolvers, pistols, airguns, and black-powder guns, plus bows, vertical or horizontal. He began formal training at age 11 during NRA sanctioned small-bore target rifle events, and became an active hunter by the age of 12. He began reloading at age 14, starting with shotgun shells and a hand-held Lee-Loader.

Steve served two combat tours in the U.S. Army while acquiring experience on numerous military firearms systems during helicopter and ground-based operations. Returning to civilian shooting, he gained further experience during NRA Bullseye, combat pistol, and shotgun competitions. These disciplines further expanded his reloading interests to metallic and shotgun ammunition.

He became an NRA-Certified Pistol, Rifle & Shotgun Instructor, and served as a certifying authority for concealed-carry permit applicants in several states. He joined the firearms industry, working with a gunsmith who was a disciple of the well-known wildcat cartridge designer, PO Ackley.

Eventually, Steve assumed control of all firearms operations for a major state agency, which included training, range operations, and equipment procurement. He holds a state criminal justice master-instructor rating, and numerous other instructor certificates. His credentials include federal, state, and manufacturer's certifications related to various firearm systems and intermediate force technologies. He has 25-plus years of full-time firearms training experience and enjoys direct contact with many industry sources.

Steve also has extensive hunting experience in the Northeast, and at other locations throughout the U.S. He holds a state archery deer record, and is author of numerous articles related to firearms and hunting.

Table of Contents

Introduction

"Firearms are second only to the Constitution in importance;
they are the peoples' liberty's teeth."
-George Washington

Disclaimer: I'm not a full-blown "Doomsday Prepper." For that matter, you may not be either. But, to some extent, I believe many people – especially many gun enthusiasts – have an underlying concern about potential future threats. What happens if somebody begins kicking in your door at 2:00 AM? If the whole system collapses, can we fend off intruders or put meat on the table? Better to have some recourse and not need it than to badly need it and not have it. For many people, firearms represent a logical recourse.

A time of tragedy is not the best time to seek a firearm. Your access to one could be restricted at any time, either by societal collapse or legislation. We've seen a glimpse of possible things to come as a result of just one event. The Newtown, Connecticut shooting tragedy stood the whole firearms supply on its head, quite literally, overnight. Some of the Second Amendment rights we took for granted were suddenly in question. Prices spiraled upward on fears of restrictive legislation and many items, particularly certain, if not most types of ammunition, were just plain unavailable. If you sense the need to build a household gun battery, *now* is the time to do it, *not* when you need it.

Filling a 24-gun safe with a fully developed collection of special-purpose firearms would be fun, but most of us don't have that financial luxury. Even if we could, we would still have the myriad types of other survival equipment and gear to accumulate: knives, optics, food, water filtration, camo-duds, cold-weather clothing, etc. Don't forget ammo, either. Add it all up and you've quickly spent a small fortune.

THE PREMISE OF THIS BOOK

This book is the first firearms book in the PrepSmart© series that will help you cover the basics of building a firearm battery. We'll buy a gun safe properly sized for our needs, and then add firearms and accessories to it, using a planned process. To help us make the best choices, we'll need to understand some underlying principles. From there, we can work toward the goal of a *coordinated* battery, beginning with just a short list of "essential systems" that constitute a base-line inventory. We can start with a shotgun, two rifles, and a handgun. Later on, we might decide to add some extras, including specialty firearms and accessories.

Our premise is built on starting with a clean slate. Many of you may already own some guns and, speaking from experience, the tendency will be to weave what you already own into the mix. While this strategy may make sense economically, overall results may be less than ideal – and in some cases, fall well short of the mark.

We'll give the essentials list a quick look here, using it primarily as an example of a planned, but practical collection. The firearms on this list, as well as many other types, will be thoroughly covered in an upcoming series of system-specific manuals. In each, the various models, ammunition and accessories will be closely examined.

While this book and the manuals are written for beginners, those familiar with firearms should find topics of value. The information will be detailed, covering far more than just the firearm itself.

Chapter 1: Selection Criteria: Some Basic Guidelines

Within each firearm system lie dozens of possible options. Where to start? Compounding the issue, some folks might be interested in defense, while others might be geared toward hunting. Many will consider both. Some common features (as well as skills) may apply to either or both. Careful selection will provide an inventory capable of fulfilling both roles. To help sort through this, I've identified some hard-nosed criteria:

Whatever we're looking at must be in widespread use. This generally rules out any recent introductions. It takes time for new ideas to catch on, and a teething process often follows a debut. I'm certainly not adverse to new ideas. My firearms training unit procures test & evaluation samples (T&E) on a regular basis, some of which are great products, but some of which are not. Well-established firearms have plenty of history behind them and will hold few surprises. Widespread use is an indicator of numerous desirable traits, and pretty much sets the stage for the following requirements.

It's got to be something with a solid reputation for dependability. We had a visit from a well-known and heavily sponsored tactical operation. They were intent on securing contracted training, and this was their second visit in as many years. During the first trip, an impressive traveling display contained an arsenal of Mossberg shotguns, which were well-equipped for the mission at hand. Although not in our inventory, we recognized the M-500 as a viable choice – especially in the tactical configuration presented to us. Less than 24 months later, the Mossbergs were gone, replaced by a stable of new and radical wonder-guns. They certainly looked cool with their unusual design and sinister appearance. Most of our tactical members were gaga over the rack of Ninja blasters. Meanwhile, the older and somewhat cynical firearms cadre looked on with cautious interest. During a subsequent demonstration, more problems were noted in six hours than we experienced with our aging Remington M-870s in a decade. A large inventory of well-used weapons provides reliable data and is the source of most recommendations.

It must be easy to operate. After playing with the unusual T&E alley-sweeping shotgun, we realized any operators would need to be restricted exclusively to this system. We'd seen more complicated firearms, but this one certainly wasn't simple. The controls were different, as was its overall operation. All of these issues could be overcome with adequate training, but only through a lot of training. Disparate function is never a good thing during stressful circumstances. Simple is better; fewer parts offer less opportunity for breakage. But, even the simplest systems will quit working at some point, so…

Parts must be readily available. Many moons ago, halfway around the world, I was having a bad spell with an unhappy enemy force intent on sharing the same piece of real estate. Because Murphy's Law, that anything that can go wrong will go wrong, is immutable, my M-2 carbine's gas-piston decided to go on vacation. Luckily, it was dark and I was able to discretely hunker down while more suitably armed comrades restored order with their issued M-16s. I had captured the M-2 and liked its controllable select-fire, cyclic-rate. The trouble was, I couldn't find a replacement piston for all the tea in China. The M-2 is just a select-fire version of the famous M-1 Carbine, an iconic U.S. World War II weapon produced in huge quantities. While some had dribbled into far-flung places, most were clearly elsewhere. Eventually, I wrote home and received a new piston from my father, who purchased it at a gun shop in New Jersey. Within a mere two months, I was back in business.

Jumping back to the Ninja shotgun mentioned above, we worried about its long-term prospects. If it flopped, parts would dry up, leaving us with a rack full of useless ornaments. On the other hand, our aging M-870 shotguns are but a few of the 10 million-plus that have been in continuous production since 1950. Using a proven system, you can predict which parts are likely to fail. From there, you can stock up on key spare parts.

A rack of Remington Model 870s, still going strong after two decades.

Ammunition must be widely available. You can't go wrong with an established military caliber like the 5.56mm (.223 Remington), 7.62x51 NATO (.308 Winchester), 9x19 (9mm Luger), or the venerable .45 ACP. Just about any hardware store with an FFL will have .22 Long Rifle, .30/06, or 12 gauge shotgun shells on hand. The same cannot be said for equally effective ammunition like the .204 Ruger, .300 SAUM, .357 Sig, .45 GAP, or 16 gauge. If you need to scrounge or barter, tip the odds in your favor. When you're buying, mainstream choices will just about always be cheaper. You'll also benefit from a much wider selection of loads to match your specific requirements.

(L) Uncommon.357 Sig, .300 SAUM & 16 Gauge. (R) Common 12 Gauge, .223 & 9mm.

It must be easy to maintain. Although this probably goes without saying, it can be easy to forget. I once bought a higher-end semi-automatic .30/06 for a bargain price. The rifle was in great shape, but I decided to give it a good cleaning prior to the first range session. I never did fire so much as a single shot from it. Disassembly and reassembly were enough of a bother that I didn't care to repeat the process. It promptly went to a new owner. Compared to more modern designs, even the immortal U.S. Government Model 1911 .45 pistol can be somewhat aggravating. I've carried one in bad places and owe my life to the gun. With several 1911s still on hand, I'm no stranger to this weapon. But, field-stripping is more complicated than John Browning's follow-up design, the P-35 High Power (which was used by both Allied and Axis forces during WWW II).

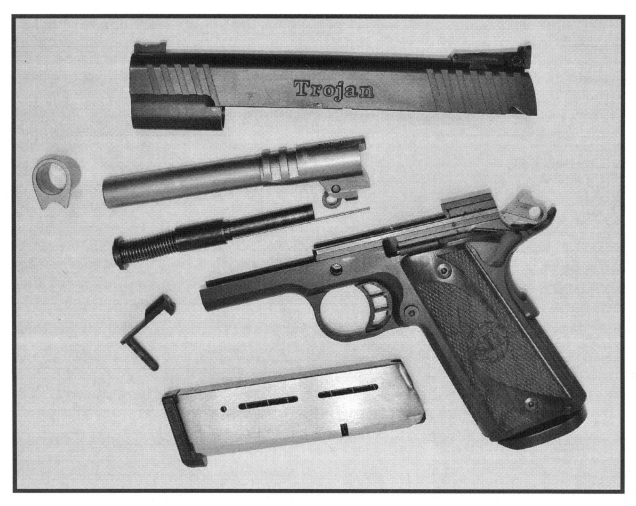

One version of the immortal 1911 in field-stripped form.

Function is crucial in a survival situation. A number of quality pistols are out there and the final choice just boils down to personal preference. Just don't forget the maintenance factor. A combination of fool-proof servicing and weather-proof construction really helps. Good walnut and polished bluing may be esthetically pleasing, but synthetic stocks and stainless-steel are what I'll reach for during rough weather.

It should accommodate practical accessories. The above-mentioned, venerable 1911 pistol is a poster-child for add-ons. The G.I. version I carried in battle was a Spartan and an archaic example of today's offerings. Most current iterations have features that were strictly custom 30 years ago; better sights and grip-safeties come to mind. Nowadays, the sky is pretty much the limit and a real concern involves knowing where to draw the line. We can tailor our 1911 to our preferences, developing a variant that meets our needs perfectly.

A modern rendition of the old war-horse Government Model 1911, shown "cocked & locked.

The AR-15 rifle is another such system with military origins, offering possibilities never imagined by the designers. A third example of an easily accessorized firearm is Ruger's 10/22 rimfire rifle. All have been widely produced for 50 years or longer and each can be tweaked by an owner using a minimum number of tools. Again, we need to be careful not to go overboard. That said, it's nice to have some practical options.

An accessorized Ruger 10/22 with popular bells and whistles.

It must represent good value. The well-known rule of thumb is to buy the best equipment you can afford; however, when it comes to firearms, "equipment" means more than just a gun.

Looking at a rifle, scope, mounts, sling, case, and ammo will jack up the final price. It's not uncommon to see higher-end rifles with lower-end scopes. *Don't go there.* All components should be serviceable and that can take some budgeting. Adding up the essentials creates a figure constituting your real bottom line. Better to skip some pieces than buy the whole package with marginal gear. That said, higher prices won't dictate "best" as it applies here. We're looking for reliable and practical items; not junk, but not gold-plated ornaments either.

Chapter 2: Knowledge, Skills, and Abilities

In the world of training, we call these "KSAs." Bringing a group of new shooters to some functional level of ability involves the design of a practical training program. By breaking the process down to key elements, we can flesh out the necessary steps. Even if you've never had any formal firearms training, you may have been through a similar process during driver education. Using a handgun as a similar example, let's consider the following:

Judgment. All bets are off without it. Either you have it or you don't. One litmus test may be your driving record. It's possible to do a lot of damage with a gun or a vehicle. If your driving history is sketchy, odds for proper observation of necessary firearms requirements aren't good either. On the other hand, assuming you've managed to get from point A to B without notable incidents, you should be able to handle the next essential requirement.

Safety. We'll spend a bit of time on this, shortly. For now, it boils down to strictly following a set of established guidelines whereby we'll responsibly manage the direction in which our firearm is pointed *at all times*. We don't run red lights or drive on the other side of a yellow line. We can't cut corners when handling guns, either.

System Proficiency. Assuming we're learning how to use a pistol, we'll need to be totally comfortable with its operation. Inexperienced drivers have accidents. On the other hand, experienced drivers may be able to steer and power their way out of skids. The subconscious mind already knows where the gas pedal and brake are located. That's where we'll need to be with the pistol. We'll need to be able to draw, engage and reload with our conscious attention directed towards threats. Once we're at that point, we can employ strategies, tipping the odds in our favor.

Tactics. When system proficiency exists, we can focus on driving to maneuver through hazards. Using similar principles with a pistol, we can quickly draw, move to cover, manage our ammunition supply, and take any other steps necessary to counter threats. With proper training, the operational aspects can occur using only the subconscious mind, thereby freeing us to formulate effective tactics. The less fortunate will still be struggling with basic operation and marksmanship – a major and possibly costly, disadvantage.

Mindset. Okay, we are driving again. We know not everyone sharing the road has it together. So we drive defensively. We're alert for any hazards and we're well-grounded in the elements listed above. We'll avoid many catastrophes by recognizing the potential problem in advance, and taking appropriate actions. This last piece is critical; it keeps us alive.

Before we go further, let's think about what we just covered. Would any of us feel comfortable jumping behind the wheel without any guidance and training? Like operating a vehicle, proper firearms handling is a huge responsibility. Based upon our actions, the lives of others hang in the balance. Others may include your immediate family, so you must get this right.

SYSTEM PROFICIENCY: An analysis

As you can see, there is more to effective employment of a firearm than might first meet the eye. We've mentioned judgment and safety. It's time to define proficiency. We might hear that someone is "good" with a handgun. What, exactly, does *that* mean? Since our frame of reference is survival-based, let's boil it down to some key pieces:

Holster skills. We won't travel with a pistol in our hand, so we'll need the ability to rapidly produce it. A number of factors come into play, including holster design, clothing, and safe, but swift techniques. Single-hand access should be considered, as well as re-holstering. It's easier than you think to shoot yourself with the wrong technique or holster.

Reloading skills. Your handgun is not belt-fed. You should avoid running out of ammo, or at least recognize when it *has* gone empty. At that point, a very speedy reload is recommended. Ammo and equipment management will come into play; picture loading an empty magazine, or trying to seat one backwards.

Use of cover. Statistics prove that a mediocre shot who takes advantage of cover will outlive a great shot that doesn't. The trick is to get as much of you as possible behind something bulletproof. The "something" may be irregularly-shaped, requiring contorted positions for best possible protection. This is not an ideal time to discover a needed reload can't be reached.

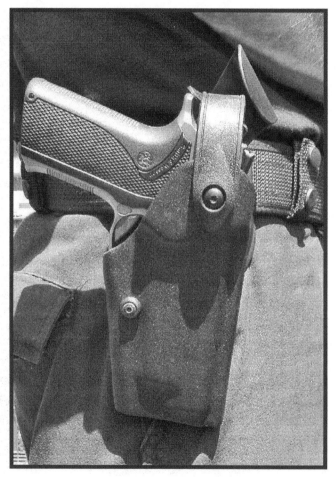

Marksmanship. The object is to make hits, but here's the problem: a gunfight isn't like shooting cans off a log. In fact, it's pretty terrifying, which explains a very low incidence of hits. The average shootout occurs inside 7 yards, and many are even closer. Right now, hit probability from trained personnel averages less than 20%. That's less than one out of five rounds hitting an adversary anywhere at all! The "trained personnel" have probably fired a multi-day course consisting of several hundred rounds or more. Unless you have magical powers, is it logical to assume you'll do better with NO training? Turn out the lights or take a hit to a hand and things can get *very* interesting. Your adversary is probably moving, and you may be, too.

Two key holster features: a covered trigger guard, and secure retention.

TRAINING

Bottom line: We need some professional guidance. Books and videos have some value. You'll see some system-specific training recommendations assigned to each manual. They can serve as a starting point but, although self-administered practice is better than nothing, we need some hands-on, relevant training to gain true proficiency.

Training examples: Sticking with our handgun theme, two civilian training sources are short, concealed-carry courses running several hours, and more in-depth, multi-day defensive schools. The former will focus on firearm safety, with a smattering of storage cautions, and possibly a bit of non-holster shooting. The latter will delve into tactics, integrating the skills identified above. Hopefully, the students will receive training on low-light techniques and shooting decisions.

I'd recommend both training options, with the former being a good starting point. The NRA is a great source, and gun clubs or local concealed-carry permit authorities will often have a list of contacts. Cost is usually reasonable. It is money well-spent, particularly for someone with limited experience.

State-run hunter safety courses can be valuable for basic shotgun and rifle training. They're normally oriented toward young hunters or inexperienced adults. The premise is similar to "Driver's Education", with basic information intended to prevent accidents. In many states, a Hunter Safety Certificate is a prerequisite to obtaining an adult hunting license. Course-length varies, but many run two days. Focus is on general long-gun handling with some field-craft thrown in. Cost is usually reasonable and attendance is worthwhile.

A more in-depth defensive school is a horse of a different color. Serious commitments will be necessary, including time, tuition, gear, and ammunition. Travel, lodging and meals may be involved as well. Shop carefully before committing, and seek references. Be wary of so-called "instructors" wearing lots of patches and pins. Schools are springing up everywhere and, while some are very good, others are questionable. Given the expense, thorough research is justified. Is such an investment worthwhile? Heck, yes! It's what we don't know that can get us in trouble. In this case, the trouble can be very bad.

Getting down and dirty: a basic rifle program.

Speaking of trouble, an "accident" involving firearms has justifiably bad connotations. One must understand the rules of the road before getting behind the wheel.

Chapter 3: Firearms Safety

I was standing by a display table at an area gun show, eyeballing a pretty double-barreled hammer gun. Two older gentlemen to my right noted my interest. The closer one turned to his companion and quietly said, "That's how Uncle Harold died." As it turned out, poor old Harold reached for his external-hammer 12 gauge shotgun after beaching his boat. The gun was propped on a seat with its barrels elevated. Harold latched on and pulled the gun towards him by the barrels. A hammer caught on the seat, came part way back and then snapped forward. Uncle Harold took a high-brass load of number fours amidships and that was that. Too bad he didn't remember a cardinal rule: Never point a firearm at something you don't intend to shoot.

Wired for safety? We've all seen stories about guns that "accidentally discharged." Cock a loaded 1911 pistol with its safety off and lay it on a table. Next, grab a seat (you'll need one) and wait for it to "accidentally discharge." Think you'll be there a while? Lock the room, return in 50 years, and you'll probably still be looking at a cocked and loaded pistol. That is, unless somebody did something stupid.

Indulge me for a moment. You, or your associates, may not be as safe with firearms as you think. It's easy to determine if you're willing to be brutally honest. Just carefully observe the relationship of the business-end of any firearms being handled by those around you. If, at any time, it points in anyone's direction (including you), unacceptable gun handling has occurred.

Here's the most disturbing concern: The problem doesn't seem to even register with a good many folks. Even those taking exception with this statement may very well sweep parts of themselves shortly after taking possession of a firearm. We see it all the time, frequently by so-called "experienced" sportsmen, who will be the first to cast aspersions upon nimrods or weekend shooters. The initial hunter safety program I attended was a classic example. Entering a large hall, two tables full of firearms were laid out and every one was pointed directly at the audience. My kids were stunned. The two subsequent events I saw were only slightly better. In all three programs, the instructors solemnly preached muzzle-management. Really?

Most people don't even know they're doing it! Being hard-nosed, many cops are atrocious, and the same goes for military personnel. Watching satellite-channel gun shows, I've seen some well-known writers sweep themselves, and this was *after* editing. How more people don't get shot is beyond me. But, some do, and I've witnessed several incidents in person. None were pretty; all were unnecessary.

FIREARMS SAFETY RULES

We can safely enjoy the fascinating world of things that go bang by following some basic rules. One trick involves sourcing a correct set. Gun manufacturers normally include a list of safety rules with their factory packaging.

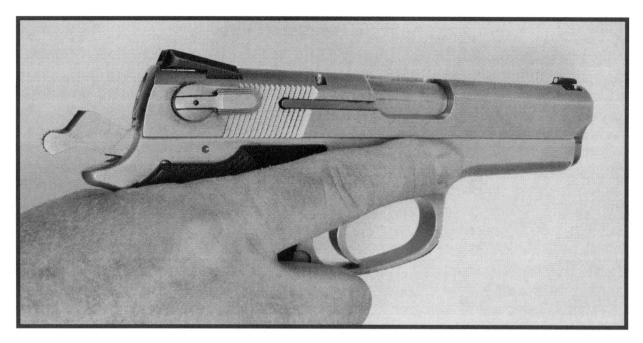

We call this Rule #3!

The **fundamental NRA Rules for safe gun handling** are required curriculum for sanctioned, basic firearms training:

1. Always keep the gun pointed in a safe direction.

2. Always keep your finger off the trigger until ready to shoot.

3. Always keep the gun unloaded until ready to use.

When using or storing a gun, always follow these NRA Rules:

- Know your target and what is beyond.

- Know how to use the gun safely.

- Be sure the gun is safe to operate.

- Use only the correct ammunition for your gun.

- Wear eye and ear protection as appropriate.

- Never use alcohol or drugs before or while shooting.

- Store guns so they are not accessible to unauthorized persons.

- Be aware that certain types of guns and many shooting activities require additional safety precautions.

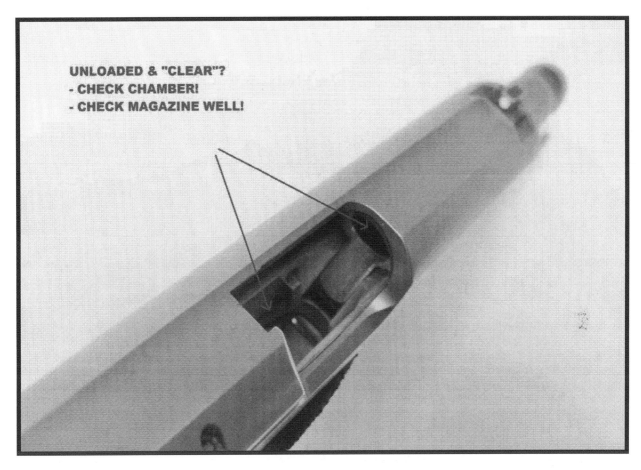

Check it, check it again!

Other versions. Different shooting schools may present proprietary rules. I deliver a two-hour firearms safety presentation during a week-long basic pistol school, and provide all shooters with a "Safety Agreement" hand-out. I'll include it here for reference. It's very similar to the NRA Rules, but we call the first five our "Universal Safety Rules." You'll often see the first four, but we added the fifth to meet our operational requirements (note #7).

Universal Safety Rules

1. Treat <u>all</u> firearms as though they are loaded, always.

2. <u>Never</u> point a firearm at anyone or anything you do not intend to <u>destroy</u>.

3. Keep your finger <u>off</u> the trigger until weapon is on target.

4. Be <u>sure</u> of your target and backstop.

5. Check it, <u>check it again.</u>

6. <u>Never</u> give a firearm to, or take a firearm from anyone, unless action is open and the firearm is unloaded.

7. If you don't know how a particular firearm operates, <u>leave it alone.</u>

8. <u>Never</u> leave a loaded firearm unattended.

9. Store firearms and ammunition separately, secure from unsupervised use.

10. Don't mix alcohol or drugs with firearms use.

General Range Safety Rules

1. <u>Always</u> point firearms in the direction least likely to endanger life and property.

2. Never handle firearms with others downrange, and only handle them on the firing line, or as directed by an Instructor.

3. Actions open, loading ports visible and safeties on when firearms are not in use.

4. Never go downrange or leave the firing line before it has been declared "SAFE" by an instructor.

5. Never lean firearms in unsupported, upright positions.

6. Never allow the muzzle of a firearm to contact the ground or snow.

7. Check the bore for obstruction before firing, or after any malfunction or unusual sounding report.

8. Use only ammo designed specifically for the firearm in which it is being used, and don't mix different types of ammo.

9. Never shoot at hard surfaces or water, and never fire bullets skyward. (One exception is the use of steel targets, provided they are used in accordance with safe industry practices.)

10. Fingers will be clear of trigger guards when drawing or holstering handguns.

11. When in ready-position with any firearm, finger is on frame.

12. Hearing and eye protection is required for all personnel on the range while shooting activities are occurring.

13. Maintain awareness of locations of others on the firing line and on the range.

14. Immediately cease fire when a "Cease Fire" is called or signaled.

VIGILANCE

One phenomenon we consistently notice, after toeing the line on safety for an entire week, things start going to hell during gun cleaning. Suddenly it's all about the individual at the expense of the group. Place community cleaning gear on a bench and you'll see muzzles waving everywhere without instructor intervention. We know it's going to happen, so we don't let it. It's as if muzzle discipline is secondary to the actual cleaning process. Well, it isn't! Another hairy period involves malfunction clearances. I can't say it enough - for God's sake, THINK! It's not just about you!

Why it matters. We've all seen those aggravating "do" and "don't" lists. I'll skip the "do" and go right to some real-life examples from the "don't" category that I'm personally familiar with:

Don't try shooting a beetle off your knee with any firearm, and most particularly not with a two-barreled derringer, which incidentally fires its lower barrel first (the bug flew away).

Don't stand a jammed auto-loading rifle on its butt and heel stomp the operating handle with your hand (or head) over the muzzle.

Don't pull a shotgun from a vehicle by its muzzle. If you're very lucky, you'll be able to hitch-hike using only your left hand.

Don't twirl any handgun – especially a loaded one. If you must, please do it alone and listen to your mother: wear clean undershorts.

Don't play with your holstered revolver in a busy military airport without first coming up with a good excuse for the smoking hole in your fatigues.

Don't point your rifle at the ceiling and pull the trigger to see if it's loaded, even if you already have a good roofer on speed-dial.

Don't…well, you get the idea. People do stupid things. Some left the gene pool and some didn't. Either way, somebody learned an expensive lesson. Plan on Murphy's Law. Live long and prosper.

Get some training. Some practical hands-on experience is highly recommended. Again, the NRA, a state hunter safety course, state concealed handgun permit course or a local gun club are all good sources.

Chapter 4: The Coyote Mindset

Not everyone is wired to be a survivor. A small percentage are very good at it, another small group are very bad, and the majority of us fall somewhere in between. The best share a trait I've seen among good soldiers and cops. They're exploitative. If a situation unravels, odds are they'll quickly identify a weakness, get a toehold, and turn the situation around to their advantage. I always figured in another life such characters were coyotes – the ultimate survivors. Those on the opposite end of the spectrum may have been sheep. Personally, I'd rather share a few coyote genes during tough times, or at least hang out with those who have them.

Sheep people ("sheeple") aren't wired defensively at all, depending instead on the greater flock for their needs. If things go to hell in a handbasket, they probably won't have a plan beyond dialing 911.

Just recognizing that 911 may not always be the answer is a step in the right direction. Anybody reading this is already at that level, and probably well beyond it. Assuming we may have to fend for ourselves, the trick is to pick the appropriate tools and have the skills to use them.

Consistency and programming. Simple is good. Complexity should be commensurate with experience. Very few of us will invest huge hours in training, and here's the kicker: marksmanship is a perishable skill. In fact, so is operation. The less we practice, the more basic things will need to be. Even those shooters who are well-versed on a particular system can develop brain cramps when some unanticipated twist occurs.

I recently had an interesting conversation with a sportsman friend whom I hold in high regard. As an ardent bird hunter, Larry managed to take an entire month off, carrying his trusty over & under Browning Citori. After much shooting, bird season was over, so his bolt action rifle was uncased for deer. A nice buck bounded by at close range, but Larry couldn't make his Remington go bang. The shotgun had a tang-mounted safety so, naturally, after 30 days of constant use, that's where Larry's thumb went. Too bad his bolt action had a side-safety.

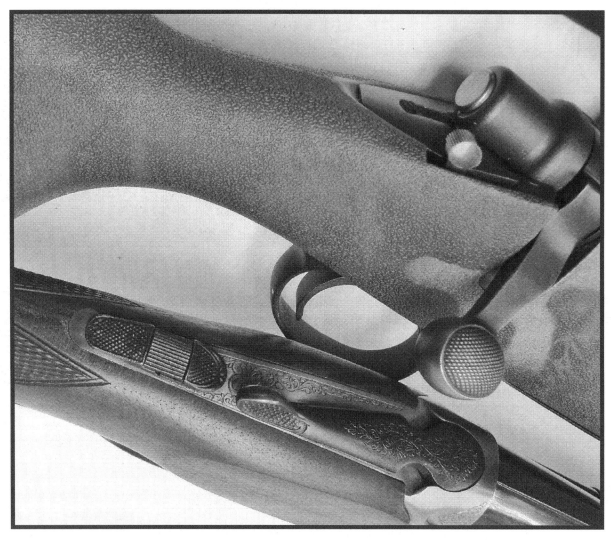

Typical safety buttons (T) Remington M-700, (B) O&U shotgun.

Programming of the subconscious mind happens through repetition, which can be a good thing – or not. For this reason, and being a creature of habit, I like to stick with firearms that share similar function. We call this a common manual-of-arms, and it could save your life in a serious social situation. With total familiarity, we can operate on auto-pilot and concentrate on our shooting.

Stress and fine motor skills. Ever hear of buck fever? It's more than just getting mixed up on the location of a safety. If you're not a hunter it goes like this: a real wall-hanger steps out and poses within easy distance, only to escape unscathed. Why? When adrenaline kicks in, the subconscious mind needs sufficient programming, or some pretty bizarre actions may occur. These can range from an entire magazine spent on wild shots, to frantic action-cycling with no shots fired at all - and a mystifying pile of live rounds scattered all over the ground. Associated symptoms involve weak knees, deep breathing, and a heavy-duty case of the shakes. Many experienced hunters have been there at some point.

While running defensive firearms programs, we often see the same effect. Fine motor skills are impaired during stress. That degrades trigger control, eroding accuracy. It then just takes something slightly off-script to completely crash shooters with marginal abilities. Add a complex manual-of-arms, poor system management or a stoppage, and operator melt-down is almost guaranteed.

True firearms competency. You may already have a handle on these issues, practicing enough to gain useful skills. If so, good! But, don't forget the unexpected. Example: do you keep a pistol for home defense? If so, is the chamber loaded? One could argue for either way. Two especially nasty individuals did a local home invasion in hopes of relieving the resident of coins. Things got ugly when the homeowner produced his pistol. At that point, one of the thugs swung a machete and nearly severed his non-gun hand. With an empty chamber, the defender had no expedient way to rack his slide. Machete blows continued. The homeowner and his young daughter were horribly mangled and left for dead. Somehow, both survived, but they were never the same.

For what it's worth, I'm a believer in the ability to operate a defensive firearm with either hand, from any position, in any light. To a lesser extent, the same applies to serious hunting endeavors. In my experience, few people are truly proficient with firearms. "Truly proficient" means the ability to run a gun on demand during any situation without conscious thought. The subconscious mind performs these tasks, freeing the conscious mind to function tactically and maintain situational control.

If things get really ugly, well-grounded shooting skills will be essential. However, perhaps somewhat surprisingly, this may constitute but half of the whole equation. We'll be busy addressing other key issues like target identification, fire and movement, ammo management, and personal composure. It's a very bad time for something to go wrong. That "something" could be an improperly latched magazine that falls out, a stoppage or an unidentified threat.

TRAINING, MURPHY'S LAW, and K.I.S.S. (Keep It Simple Stupid)

Concerning these principles, you may detect a relationship. Without the former, those disregarding the latter are destined to meet our central character, Mr. Murphy – who most assuredly will appear at the worst possible moment. It's easy to get caught up in the technology race. We're seeing AR-15s with just about every accessory short of mud-flaps or a plastic Jesus. This phenomenon is largely attributable to the "cool factor" and possibly based on a "more is better" mindset. After several days of hard and fast-paced range-work, many Rambo goodies disappear. Some just break while others are removed to restore some semblance of sanity. You can't spend your way to victory. As an example, let's consider two hypothetical and opposing forces.

The first group is well-trained, but possesses mediocre equipment. For purposes of this comparison, "mediocre" doesn't mean junk. It might just be dated, consisting of WWII weapons, or possibly even older items from the late 1800s. Let's assume these troops have a high level of proficiency with firearms, and are well-versed in tactics. They appreciate the limitations imposed by their equipment and have cohesively trained to maximize their effectiveness.

The second group has state-of-the-art equipment, but mediocre training. In this case, the equipment might be the equivalent of modern U.S. military infantry weapons like an M-4. However, possibly due to a 'Rambo' attitude, less effort has been expended on the training aspects. Belief in superiority of equipment provides a false sense of security.

Which is likely to prevail? I'll bet on the first group. Interestingly, when calculating the overall costs of equipment and training, the totals might not be much different. At this point, you may be thinking while this is fine and good, no platoon-size group of allies will likely be available for support. A logical solution would be to increase personal fire-power. It's a valid concept - to a point. But sheer volume of fire by itself won't always solve a problem.

Toys versus talent. For the record, I'm far from the most talented shootist out there. Knowing my limits, I tend to proceed with a mixture of caution, combined with the KISS principle.

I'll never forget an interesting competition between me and a very good shooter named Dave who was armed with a select-fire 9mm submachine gun. I had a .45 ACP 1911 pistol and our challenge was to engage an array of five steel plates located at various distances from 10 to 25 yards. The first one to knock down all five won, three runs determined the winner. With only a seven-round magazine, but plenty of government-model experience, I figured my best bet was to fire at a controlled pace. My opponent's SMG held 32 rounds. He came in second all three times. Dave was getting cranky so we threw in two more runs. The outcome didn't change, but it did illustrate a well-known premise: spray and pray just isn't all that effective. Adding insult to injury, the buzz-gun shooter burned through three boxes of ammo. I still had half of my first box left. If times are hard and ammo is scarce, disciplined fire will be critical.

A typical 9mm buzz-gun, which looks cool, but has an expensive diet.

Straightforward choices. Dave had lots of flashy toys and leaned towards the 'Rambo' mentality. We've all heard the phrase, "jack of all trades and master of none". That applied here. Dave seemed a bit uncomfortable with his cool-looking blaster and probably lapsed into spray-mode because of inexperience. With better training, he could've kicked my butt on semi-auto. It would have been a cheaper strategy to boot. Did I mention that my so-called Model 1911 pistol is so-named because our military adopted it in that year?

We've run a similar drill pitting two competent hand-gunners against one good lever-action shooter. Although the outcome isn't guaranteed, the rifle usually wins. It's a Marlin Model 1894 "Cowboy II", firing .38 specials – older but still reliable 19th century technology!

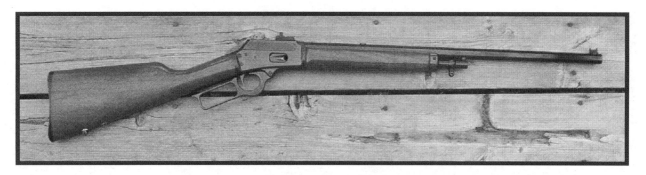

Reliable 19ᵗʰ Century technology: A Marin .357 Model 1894.

At the tail end of my agency's revolver era, most surrounding departments had already switched to semi-automatic pistols. We had pistol-envy and fiscal woes, but worked hard to reinforce the basics. We ran joint programs with shooters present from both categories on several occasions. As a whole, our revolver-shooters bested the semi-auto gang every time. Scores were higher and, surprisingly, the first shot recorded during the timed reloading stage was usually fired by a wheel-gun – in this case, an S&W double-action K-frame, which was introduced during 1899. My lead instructor, Mike, will spank just about everybody with his S&W M-686 L-frame and conventional speed-loaders. He shoots International Defensive Pistol Association (IDPA) matches in several states and usually wins not only his class, but the entire match. Because so many folks today believe a revolver is arcane, it's fun to watch.

The mention of late-1800s firearms is sure to raise an eyebrow, but have you ever watched a Cowboy Action Shoot? Period-type single-action peace-makers, lever-guns, and shotguns are standard fare. The better shooters have lots of range time and can throw serious lead down-range. Anyone on the receiving end would most likely be in a heap of trouble, no matter what they had for hand-held weapons. You really have to see it to believe it. It's downright humbling, but makes a point.

Am I suggesting we should forsake the latest technology for simple old-school designs? Not at all! However, there's more to survival than expensive equipment. The stuff we choose should be suitable for the tasks at hand, dead-nuts reliable, and operable under pressure. Let's think real life. Are we really going to invest thousands of dollars on full-blown tactical gear? Are we really going to commit to hundreds of hours for tactical training? Do we even need to do that, and do we really want to have a close relationship with those that play the part? A boonie hat and MOLLE gear provide no assurance of tactical prowess. They really won't be half as useful as a first-aid kit, cellphone, or fire extinguisher in real world circumstances.

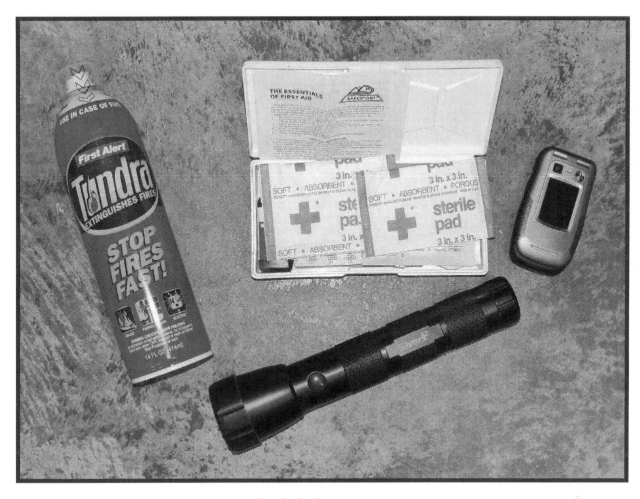

Don't overlook the basic emergency items.

We can choose practical equipment with common sense. If we back that up with relevant training and adequate practice, we'll be better-prepared to deal with Old Man Murphy when he inevitably appears.

Chapter 5: A Personal Firearms Assessment

Now that we have a handle on what's involved with serious firearm usage (and, believe me, it's all serious), we can gauge our unique situation concerning investments in firearms, equipment, training and, most importantly, commitment. Obviously those with greater resources will have more options; however, a shoestring budget doesn't put you out of the running. You just need simple and dependable stuff and, if it all works in a similar manner, so much the better. Training is easier and any practice will mutually support your entire system.

A familiar manual-of-arms and structured training will go a long way toward skill-building. As an example, between work and home, I use a collection of bolt action rifles in various calibers. These are Remington Model 700s and Model Sevens, which function identically. I can access their safety switches without conscious thought, loading or unloading them in the dark. They all have the same familiar feeling, essential during a moment of truth. Anytime I use one I obtain transferable practice with the entire system.

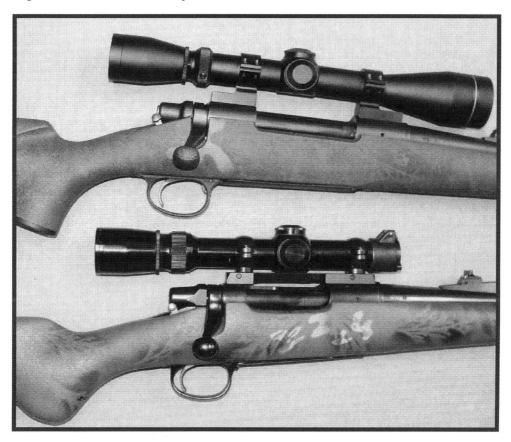

Remington M-700 (T), and M-7 (B): two different actions sharing one common function.

Some folks may not want "an entire system", being content with just a gun or two. That's fine, but the fewer guns on hand, the more versatile they should be. Regardless of quantity, reliability is equally important, as is durability. To that end, I take stainless steel whenever possible, paired with synthetic stocks. The things we depend on during rough conditions warrant durability.

The firearms we'll examine here are in widespread use, thus assuring availability of parts and accessories. When discussing a particular brand there may be other choices that are equally good. However, I'm sticking to things with which I have longstanding personal experience – stuff that works. We just need to decide how far into gun land we really want to go.

OPTIONS

Many moons ago, I'd enthusiastically wade through the giant Sears catalogs full of forbidden treasures. Pellet guns, rifles, and "Ted Williams" shotguns beckoned, along with dozens of other items consisting of, at times, boats, appliances, and even houses. I noticed three descriptive categories with implied connotations: "economy; better; and best". The economy-grade stuff, even for a kid in his mid-teens, was less than reassuring. "Sears Best" seemed like an iron-clad guarantee of quality, whereas "Better" provided some glimmer of hope without breaking the bank.

Extending this principle to our firearms battery some 50 years later, we'll look at different paths to meet our needs, depending on finances and personal interest. Here's my cross to bear: As a shooter, it's loads of fun to play with all the toys. Many come and go, but lurking in the safe is a nucleus of battle-scarred old standbys that have been through thick and thin. Interestingly, these tend to fall under the "better" category.

Those that get used the least are often referred to as safe queens. They look pretty, but that's about it. Let's stick with firearms offering real utility and learn how to shoot 'em.

Many folks are over-gunned, over-scoped, and over-choked. Too much gun leads to flinching from recoil and muzzle-blast. Too much scope magnification results in a small field of view and difficulty picking up targets. Tight chokes throw smaller shotgun patterns that result in misses at all but extreme ranges. It's hard to master anything when crippled by such impediments. Much like high fat foods and prune juice, moderation is the key.

A BASIC BATTERY

There are several firearms I wouldn't want to be without and, in order of importance, they include the following:

Shotgun. For serious social situations, this tool is just the ticket. We'll explore the scattergun in depth later on. For now, suffice to say it is one versatile firearm. The right gun and proper assortment of shells will handle everything from small game and birds to large game and home defense. I'll take a 12 Gauge, but smaller-statured users could certainly make do with a trimmer 20 Gauge model.

A 12 Gauge Remington Model 870 Express in bird-gun dress.

Rimfire rifle. Here's your basic plinking, practice, fun, and food-for-the-pot tool. Although several calibers exist, the .22 just can't be beat. Ammo is abundant (usually), cheap, portable and fairly quiet. In fact, some of the purpose-built loads are very quiet. One can acquire a rifle and plenty of ammunition for a modest investment. Your larder can be stocked with small game from that point on. If things totally tank, while the mall crowd is desperately trying to figure out how to eat their makeup, a properly equipped prepper can rustle up a tasty dinner of gray squirrels (which, incidentally, *do* taste like chicken).

A Remington Model 504 bolt action .22 LR, squirrel ready.

Centerfire rifle. This firearm, in a well-proven caliber like .30/06 or .308, is the rifle reserved for heavy hitting. It'll be loud and cartridges won't be cheap, but you'll be able to tackle game as large as moose. The calibers mentioned were initially developed for military use and you can expect decisive results against two-legged invaders. Ammo is widely available in these common calibers, allowing just about any need to be met.

A Remington Model 700 .30/06, fully capable of taking larger game. Note the functional similarities to its smaller .22 cousin.

Centerfire handgun. Whether intended for concealed carry or close-quarter self-defense, a reasonably portable sidearm has value. Choose the right type and you can even harvest game in a pinch. You'll want something with adequate power and manageable recoil, without excessive size or weight. Options boil down to either a double-action revolver, or a semi-automatic pistol. Either will suffice, but the versatile .357 Magnum is a great revolver pick. It will also fire milder .38 Special rounds and is an easy system to master, although capacity will be less than a pistol. Those preferring a pistol should look at 9mm, .40 S&W, or .45 ACP, depending on their physical stature. Although a bit more complicated, ammo-capacity will be greater. There are many handgun choices, but if I was limited to one, it would be a good, double-action revolver.

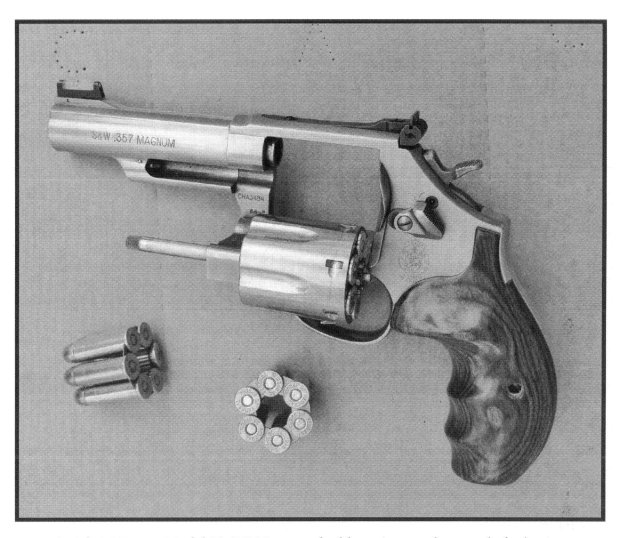

A Smith & Wesson Model 66 .357 Magnum double action revolver, ready for business.

More on handguns. Say what? No high-capacity wonder-pistol? Everybody needs to breathe in a paper bag for a minute and listen up. Until around 1985, .357 Magnum revolvers reigned as the preeminent choice among lawmen throughout America. It's still a completely viable option capable of digesting all sorts of .38 Special and .357 Magnum loads. A wide range of power-levels is thus available and, unlike a semi-auto pistol, if you can stuff a cartridge in and close the action, a wheel-gun will fire and function with great reliability. A quality gun like a stainless, four-inch barreled S&W Model 66 (or 686) will even carry well, working reliably in the harshest conditions. It's also a user-friendly choice. Adjustable sights can be regulated to place various loads accurately to point of aim. Using speed-loaders, with proper training, those unfamiliar with the system will be very surprised to see just how fast a reload can happen.

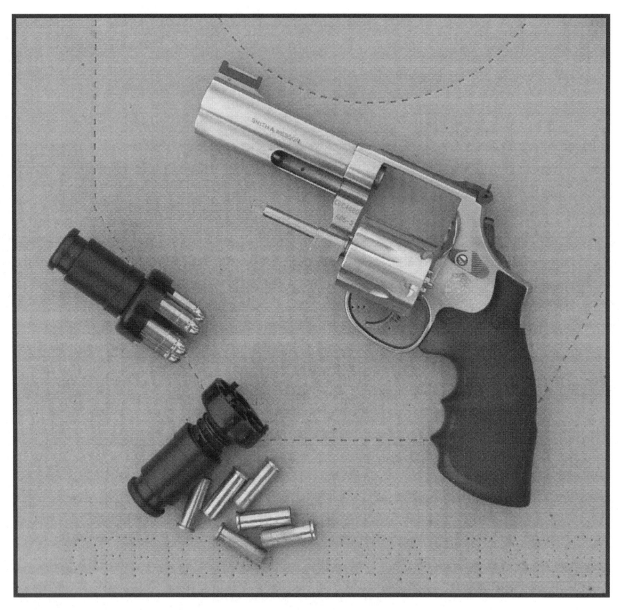

An S&W M-686 with Safariland speedloaders. Reloads are fast!

The .357 is the gold-standard when comparing other handgun calibers used for self-defense. Carefully chosen loads will also handle game up to the size of deer, and .38 Special rounds work well on small game. In other words, it's one heck of a versatile handgun! Not that a pistol is a bad choice – it isn't. Many of the attributes just mentioned apply to a carefully selected semi-auto, and options abound, so the hardest part might be nailing the final selection. Still, for complete versatility and overall simplicity, balanced against training requirements, a revolver will more than suffice.

Systems and affordability. Are you surprised to see no in-depth mention of a Glock or 1911 pistol? Remember, this is a pragmatic and bare-boned "economy" list. How about the lack of an AR-15? All would be worthwhile additions but, truthfully, there is very little that couldn't be accomplished with a basic firearms battery.

For practical purposes, a firearm, whether a shotgun, rifle or handgun, is just one part of an overall system. A good example is that AR-15 rifle. Weapon cost won't be cheap, and it won't do you much good without a few other essential items. These include spare magazines, a sling and case, cleaning gear, a few key parts, and an optical sight with mount. Adding the costs of the firearm and necessary items will give you the system cost. In some cases, this figure will be quite a bit more than the base-line gun. Randomly picked firearms can quickly escalate costs, running your wallet dry. As a result, you can wind up with incomplete systems that are less effective.

An AR-15 and some, but not all, of the system's components.

We can minimize our system costs through honest assessment. The forthcoming "basic firearms battery" you'll see shortly lacks the tactical glitz of some popular guns, but won't break the bank with expensive extras.

We're swapping out "tactical" for "practical." *Don't forget, you'll still need ammunition!*

This stash of ammo isn't really that big, but it sure isn't cheap!

Chapter 6: A Tutorial on Ammunition

Firearms aficionados have their own jargon. Calibers and ammunition are frequent topics, with various types bandied about. The assumption is that everyone will understand a reference to something like a "twenty-two", or other common firearm. For the uninitiated, what do numbers like .22, .30/06, or 12 gauge actually mean?

Sporting ammunition generally falls under two categories: metallic and shotshell. The .22 and .30/06 cartridges are examples of metallic ammunition. The 12 gauge is a shotshell.

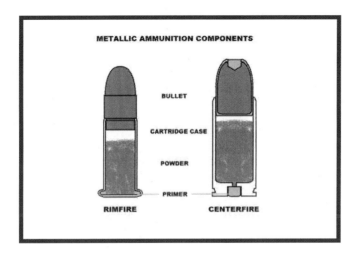

Metallic ammunition designs: rimfire & centerfire cartridges.

CARTRIDGE NOMENCLATURE

Let's start with that .22 caliber firearm. It fires a very small cartridge, which generates little noise or recoil. Like other, larger designs, the "cartridge" itself is composed of four key components:

Live and disassembled .22 LR cartridges, shown with a fired case (note the indented rim).

Bullet. This is the actual projectile and is typically made out of lead, a dense and malleable material. It may or may not be encased in a thin copper jacket (hence the term "full metal jacket"). Its diameter will normally be expressed in "calibers", and its weight will be measured in "grains." A .22 bullet is normally a plain lead alloy, although it may be coated with a very thin copper wash. More potent, high-velocity loads utilize a thicker jacket to prevent lead accumulations inside the barrel. The profile of the bullet and jacket design can either prevent or promote expansion in a controlled manner, depending on the intended application.

Cartridge case. Normally made out of brass, it serves as a container, holding the bullet and a powder charge. Upon discharge, its ductile walls expand to contain rearward pressure. Once the bullet exits the barrel, the case shrinks a bit to permit extraction. A .22 rimfire case is made from very thin brass and, due to its priming design, becomes disposable after firing. Larger centerfire cartridges, which develop greater pressure, are usually much thicker. Depending on their priming system, they may be salvageable for reloading with new components. Some ammunition is made with aluminum or mild steel cartridge casings. They are generally more affordable, but also non-reloadable.

Powder. Otherwise known as a propellant, modern "smokeless" powder rapidly burns, instead of exploding. When confined, its ignition produces high-pressure gas, expelling a projectile with great force. There are many types of powders that burn at different rates. They should not be confused with the original "black powder" propellant, which remained in use for ten centuries. Black powder behaves more like an explosive, emitting large volumes of corrosive, sulfurous smoke. Our more efficient and non-corrosive smokeless powders appeared during the late 1800s, quickly supplanting black powder. Today, use of black powder is primarily confined to period-piece firearms.

Primer. This small explosive charge is located in the rear of the cartridge, and is struck by a gun's firing pin. The resulting flash ignites the main powder charge. In our aptly-named .22 "rimfire" cartridge, a priming mix is spun into its annular rim. A blow from the firing pin pinches the brass rim against the compound, causing detonation. A "centerfire" cartridge contains a separate primer located in the center of cartridge base. The American "Boxer" design is self-contained, lending itself to reloading. The European "Berdan" system works differently, and is difficult to reload.

Live & fired cartridges: rimfire .22 (L), centerfire .223 (R).

<u>Non-metallic ammunition.</u> Shotshells work in a similar manner, but typically fire multiple projectiles. As such, the 'bullet' will be a payload of small shot pellets, contained within a plastic wad-cup. The "cartridge" (which runs at comparatively lower pressure), will be a thin-walled plastic tube with a metal base. It will be ignited by a larger "battery cup" centerfire primer, and can often be reloaded.

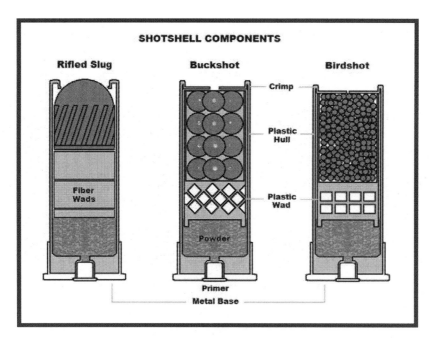

Typical shotshell designs: slug, 00 buckshot & birdshot.

While metallic ammunition is cataloged by calibers (or millimeters), shotshells are sized as gauges, the 12 gauge being the most popular. A 10-gauge is bigger and the 16, 20, 28 & .410-bore are all smaller. In fact, the .410 isn't really a gauge at all. This information is thoroughly covered in the shotgun manual that accompanies this series.

12 Ga., 20 Ga., .410 bore shell bases. Note their head-stamps and relative sizes.

CALIBERS, MILLIMETERS, AND GAUGES

Although the uninformed will sometimes refer to a loaded cartridge as a "bullet", they are really just describing one part of a cartridge. The assembled cartridge is commonly referred to as a "round." Other terms will serve to quantify its type, size and capabilities.

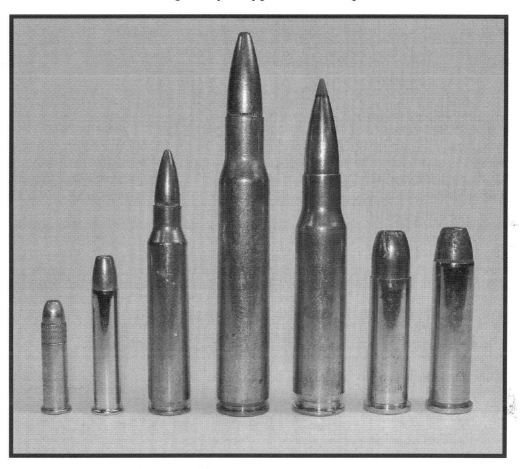

The cartridge line-up, covered below (L – R): .22 LR, .22 WMR, .223, .30/06,
308, .38 Special, .357 Magnum.

<u>**Caliber (Cal.).**</u> A caliber equals one one-hundredth (0.01") of an inch. Thus, a .22-caliber bullet is roughly twenty-two one hundredths of an inch (0.22") in diameter. I use the term "roughly" because great license has been used by firearms manufacturers when labeling new cartridges. There are plenty of different .22-caliber cartridge listings, in both rimfire and centerfire persuasions. The true diameter may vary from its label. The most popular rimfire load is the .22 Long Rifle (.22 LR). Its true diameter is 0.0223.

The hotter .22 Magnum measures 0.0224, and uses a longer, straight-walled case of greater diameter. These rounds are similar in design, but are not interchangeable (although a few revolvers are sold with both cylinders). Firing a .22 LR in a larger-diameter .22 Magnum (WMR) chamber is unsafe.

The more powerful .223 Remington uses a somewhat heavier bullet of the same .224 diameter, but has a larger, bottle-necked case of centerfire design. The similar M-16 cartridge is known as a 5.56mm, but should not be fired in a .223 Remington chamber.

A .30/06 is much larger, and but one of many thirty-caliber cartridges firing a .308-diameter bullet. Here's where things get strange: the '06 refers to the year this round was adopted by the U.S. Army. It's also called the "ought-six", or "thirty ought-six" Springfield.

The .308 Winchester fires the same diameter bullet to a similar velocity, but is a shorter and more modern version. The military calls it a 7.62x51 NATO.

A .38 Special really measures 0.357". The famous .357 Magnum is a longer version, loaded to higher pressure. You can safely fire a .38 Special in a .357 Magnum revolver, but not in reverse order.

The whole thing can be very confusing for beginners and, since most loads are not interchangeable, you can get in serious trouble by firing an incorrect round. If in doubt, first check with a trustworthy source!

Millimeter (mm). The metric cartridge system is much more logical, although still imperfect. One millimeter (mm) equals roughly four calibers, so a 9mm is approximately .36-caliber (.355). The question is: which 9mm? There are several to choose from. The very popular 9mm Luger is a 9x19mm, and the second number refers to the length of its cartridge case. It is different than the shorter 9x17mm, otherwise known as a .380 ACP (or 9mm Kurz). In military parlance, the .308 Winchester is a 7.62x51 NATO round. The smaller Soviet load is a 7.62x39mm Russian (which actually fires .311 bullets). The 5.56mm NATO will fire .223 Remington ammo, but as previously mentioned, the reverse may be unsafe. Again, you need to be sure of what you're firing!

The 7.62x39 Russian (L), and 7.62x51 NATO (R). In civilian terms the NATO cartridge is known as the .308 Winchester.

Gauge (Ga.). This old English system is used to quantify the internal diameter of shotgun barrels. "Gauge" is determined by the number of round, lead balls that will squeak through a barrel and equal a pound. In the case of a 16-gauge, the number of lead balls is 16, meaning each will weigh an ounce. For that reason, shotgun payloads are expressed in ounces, rather than grains. The "payload" will be a column of shot pellets, ejected as an expanding swarm. A standard 16-gauge shell throws one ounce of shot, and the larger, highly popular 12 gauge standard load is 1 1/8 ounces. The smaller 20-gauge standard is 7/8 ounce. These weights now vary considerably, and many 12 gauge loads approach 2 ounces. Shotgun shells are listed by length, with 2 ¾" being common. The 16 is now semi-obsolete, although the 20 prospers. Its heavier, 3" magnum payloads explain the decline of the bigger-bore "sixteen." The many facets of this topic are explained further in the shotgun manual that accompanies this series.

OTHER TERMS

Chamber. Ammunition must occupy a close-fitting space to safely contain the severe pressures generated upon discharge. The ductile cartridge can then expand to seal the rear (or breech) end of the barrel. Inserting a loaded cartridge (or shotgun shell) into a firearm is often described as "chambering" a round. A barrel will usually be marked for its chamber, whether caliber, millimeter, or gauge.

This Marlin's .22 LR barrel is clearly marked. If you're not sure what you have,
don't attempt to load or fire it!

Magnum. This somewhat nebulous term is used to describe a cartridge with extra power. "Magnum" may be applied to a stretched-out version of a standard load, the .38 Special and its hotter .357 Magnum offspring being good examples. Although both are the same diameter, the .357 uses a slightly longer cartridge case and is loaded to much greater pressure. Higher velocity is attained, but recoil is more pronounced.

.38 Special (L) and .357 Magnum (R). Note the slightly longer cartridge case of the .357.
The shorter .38 Special can be safely fired in a .357 Magnum chamber – but not the reverse!

Magnum shotgun shells are designed similarly with standard 2 ¾" and 3" Magnums being the norm. Some metallic magnum calibers may be based on entirely different cartridges. The .300 Winchester Magnum fires bullets of the same .308 diameter as a .30/06 or .308, but uses a larger case with more propellant to achieve greater velocity.

<u>Grains.</u> We can use this unit of measurement to quantify the weight of a bullet. It's also used by reloaders to determine a powder charge weight, and should not be confused with individual grains of powder. As a unit of weight, there are 7,000 grains in a pound and 437.5 grains in an ounce. A standard .22 LR bullet weighs only 40 grains. A 55-grain military 5.56mm bullet is just a

bit heavier, but travels at a much higher velocity. A common 9mm bullet weighs 115-grains, whereas a .45 ACP is double that, or 230 grains. Cartridges like the .30/06 Springfield or .308 Winchester often use bullets weighing 150 grains. A standard 12 gauge shotgun slug (which is a .73-caliber bullet) weighs an ounce. More mass may mean more terminal punch, but velocity is also important.

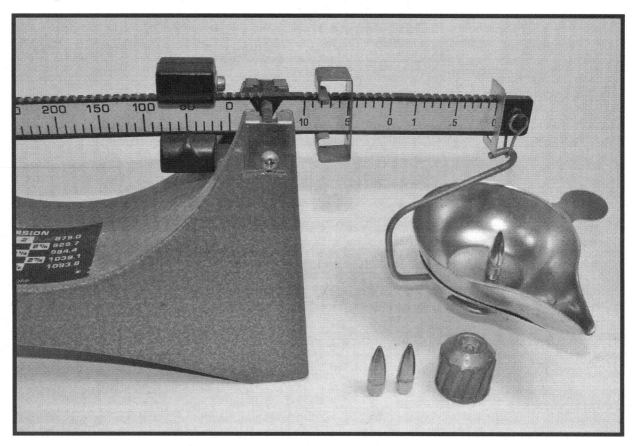

This reloading scale indicates the .223 bullets weighs 55-grains.
The big 12 Ga. slug should weigh about 437.5 grains, or one ounce.

Muzzle velocity (MV). The speed at which a projectile exits a barrel (its muzzle) is expressed in feet per second (fps). This data is usually recorded around 15 feet off the muzzle, using a chronograph.

A chronograph, displaying velocity in feet-per-second.
In this case, a lightweight 40-grain .223-bullet clocked impressive speed.

Modern cartridges have quite a spread, from below 1,000 fps, up to 4,000 fps or more. A .22 LR will start out slightly above 1,000 fps. Centerfire handgun MV is a bit above, or just below that speed. Rifle calibers like the .223 or .308 will start near 3,000 fps. Regardless, air resistance slows the bullet, causing decreased terminal effects and increased drop.

Muzzle energy (ME). Defining so-called "stopping power" is a difficult task due to various influences. Besides caliber and velocity, mass and bullet design are other important factors. There are several formulas to quantify terminal force, but foot-pounds (ft-lbs) of energy are most often listed. The figure is a product of projectile mass and speed, but it can be deceiving. Some state wildlife agencies mandate minimums for big game hunting calibers. You may see a requirement for an expanding bullet of at least .24-caliber, with a 1,000 ft-lbs minimum. This is one approach to help ensure humane harvest of deer or larger-sized animals. An easy thing to miss is the "expanding bullet", which will cause more tissue damage than a non-expanding type. In other words, foot-pounds alone won't provide a complete picture. While the foot-pound spread is large, running from 100 ft-lbs for a .22 LR, to centerfire rifle figures exceeding 3,000 ft-lbs, these numbers don't directly translate to actual force delivered on-target. We often see low pistol hits on knock-down silhouette targets that leave them standing. We can push them over with just one finger.

Trajectory. A common misconception is that a bullet rises above the bore axis, but it doesn't. The moment we fire a shot, gravity takes over at a constant rate. With your barrel parallel to the earth, if you dropped a rock at the same instant you fired a bullet; both would land at the same instant. So, the distance the bullet travels during that time will govern its flight-path or "trajectory." We can picture it as a parabolic curve that increases with range. Faster bullets will cover more ground during their descent, but mass and profile are other factors. Even the flattest-shooting cartridges used by long-range shooters incur significant drop as ranges extend. Wind is another big concern and both can conspire to cause misses. For most experienced hunters, a 400-yard shot is quite a poke.

BULLET TYPES

When buying ammunition, the box will list caliber, bullet weight, and type. The latter may be identified by an abbreviation, or actually spelled out. There are many types and those shown following are a few.

Just about all bullets intended for defense or big game hunting are designed to expand. Upon impact, they upset, growing larger in diameter. The bugaboo for manufacturers has been a satisfactory combination of expansion, weight-retention, and penetration. Ideally, a nicely-expanded bullet will display large "banana-peeled" petals and an unexpanded shank, resembling a mushroom. Weight will remain close to its unfired mass. Reality proves that impact with foreign objects or bone can cause core and jacket separation, or projectile disintegration. Such damage can greatly limit penetration, reducing terminal results.

This 9mm jacketed hollow-point exhibited classic expansion and good penetration in the calibrated ballistic gelatin block.

For years, most bullets were cup & core designs. They have a lead core and outer copper jacket, leaving some lead exposed at the tip. The latest "monolithic" bullets are made entirely from solid copper or bronze. When matched to their intended velocities, they expand nicely and shed little mass. Other bullets may be composite designs, using polymer tips or tungsten cores. "Bonded" bullets have lead cores soldered to copper jackets. These designs are another way to improve bullet integrity while promoting "controlled expansion." These more elaborate designs will often be referred to as "premium bullets" with cost reflecting the title.

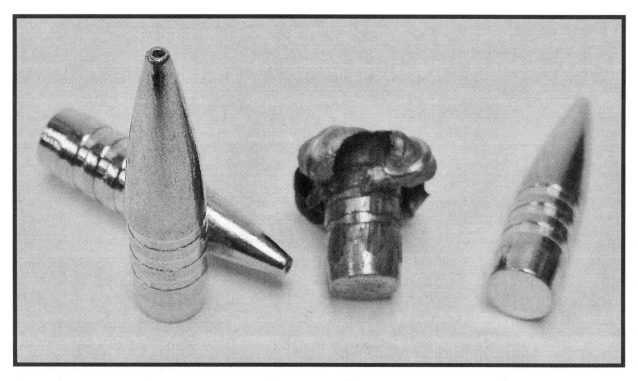

Solid-copper .30-caliber Barnes Triple-Shock bullets. The expanded TSX penetrated a big deer lengthwise, but still weighs nearly 150 grains – impressive performance!

Varmint hunters will seek fragile, high-velocity projectiles designed for "pink mist" emanating from the target. Small game hunters may be looking for just the opposite; non-destructive bullets to help minimize meat damage. Target shooters probably just need to punch a hole. The military needs non-expanding bullets to meet international law. In the end, we wind up with a huge assortment of projectiles:

FMJ stands for "full metal jacket" bullet. Typically, it will be made out of lead, encased in a thin copper sheathing. It will generally feed well in semi-automatic firearms. Expansion may be non-existent, but penetration may be deep. The Hague Convention limits signatories to FMJs, which are supposedly less destructive, explaining their widespread military use.

HP stands for "hollow point." The design is similar to an FMJ, but the bullet has a cavity in its nose. It is usually designed to expand or "mushroom" in tissue, creating a larger wound cavity and more damage, with possibly less penetration. It's a popular choice for self-defense or hunting. Some rifle HPs are designed as match bullets, unsuitable for hunting.

SP stands for "soft point", with construction similar to FMJs. However, a small portion of the nose may be exposed lead. The latest polymer-tipped rifle bullets are a hybrid JHP/SP, with a plastic nose. Either type is designed to expand after contact with tissue, making them good big game picks. Rifle bullets may also be listed with a "boat tail" (BT) profile, in which case they'll have a tapered rear section for enhanced streamlining.

RN means a "round nose" profile. The bullet may be plain lead (.22 and .38 revolver), or jacketed (9mm FMJ). Such bullets chamber easily, but cause minimal tissue damage.

TC such bullets are usually pistol types. Picture a RN with a flat tip and you'll have a "truncated cone."

SWC similar to a TC, "semi-wadcutter" bullets have a cylindrical body with a short, flat nose. They are a common centerfire revolver choice, and usually composed of lead.

WC a "wadcutter" is like a SWC, but without its tapered nose section. A WC is essentially a lead cylinder, used primarily for revolver target shooting.

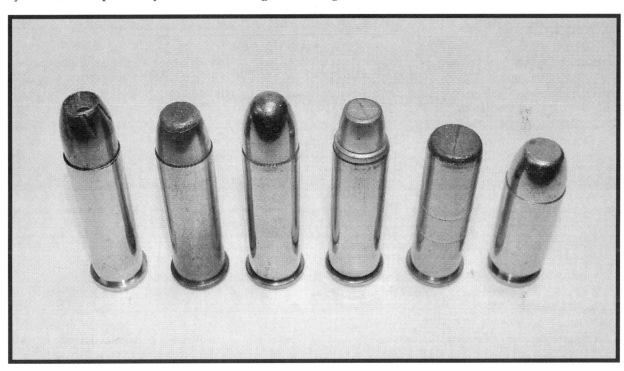

A line-up of handgun bullets (L-R): JHP, SP, RN, SWC, WC & TC. The latter is a .40 S&W.
All others are .38 Special types. The RN is also a FMJ, or full-metal-jacket.

On my desk is a box labeled "Wolf 7.62x39 mm, 122 Gr., HP Steel-Case" cartridges." From this information we can determine its manufacturer, bullet weight, and design. The steel cartridge case won't be reloadable, but it can be retrieved with a magnet!

A box of 7.62x39 Russian 122-grain HPs.
Note the steel case cartridges common to some foreign ammo.

CHOOSING CALIBERS

Newton's laws are incontrovertible. For every action there is an equal and opposite reaction. Don't believe the images portrayed by Hollywood, with bad guys blown skyward from torso hits. If you fired a weapon capable of delivering that much force, what do you suppose it would do to you? I have no personal desire to find out! A practical balance of performance and manageable recoil lays somewhere. Among a crowded field of candidates, we can narrow our survival-based options by focusing on those in widespread use.

Shotgun. A 12 gauge can fill many roles and shells are widely available. Birdshot, buckshot, or bullet-like slugs are all great options for defense or most hunting scenarios. A 2 ¾" non-magnum shell will serve very well and help reduce recoil. Small-statured users could go with a 20-gauge while maintaining adequate performance.

Three useful 12 Ga. loads in birdshot, slug & 00 Buck.
Don't rule out the #6 birdshot for close-quarter home defense.

Rimfire rifle. For practice or quiet small game hunting, the ubiquitous .22 LR is hard to beat. Beyond the standard ammo choices, some interesting loads exist. These include new "quiet" rounds that greatly minimize noise.

A diverse line-up of .22 LR loads, ranging from quiet subsonic through high-velocity rounds.
Note the tiny .22 shotshell shown on the far left.

Centerfire rifle. The .308 Winchester is a solid, all-around pick. The less powerful .223/5.56mm may have defensive value in a system like the AR-15, but it lacks the power to anchor large animals. To some extent recent, .223 offerings have improved performance, but their limited distribution is a concern. On the other hand, the .308 will handle everything. Recoil is manageable and a large selection of excellent loads exists.

The tried and true .308 "Remington Core-Lokt " is an old school and basic design, but it will still bring home the bacon (or venison).

Handguns. The well-proven .357 Magnum makes a great revolver choice. It has enough power to take a deer and is the gold standard of defensive rounds. For most people, recoil is tolerable, but if not, somewhat less powerful +P .38 Special rounds can be substituted. For practice or small game, milder, standard-velocity .38 Special ammunition may be used.

L-R: .357 Magnum, .38 Special +P, and .38 standard-velocity, all of which can be safely fired in a .357 Magnum revolver. Practice with the cheaper .38 FMJs.

Those choosing a pistol will be well-served by a 9mm, .40 S&W, or .45 ACP. The least expensive 9mm offers high capacity, mild recoil and power equivalent to a +P .38. The recent spate of excellent bullets addresses previous concerns about marginal performance. Conversely, the.45 ACP fires larger cartridges, which limit capacity and increase cost. Recoil is more pronounced, but the .45 is the benchmark for defensive pistol use. The in-between .40 S&W has been widely adopted by law enforcement agencies for good reason. It offers more power than a 9mm, less recoil than a .45, and reasonable capacity. Cost falls between the 9mm and .45.

Classic pistol cartridge choices (L-R): 9mm, .40 S&W, .45 ACP –
all shown with FMJ bullets best suited for practice.

Load selection. Our bullet choices will play as large a part as our final caliber selections. We'll need to match each to the intended task, whether plinking or hunting big game. For cans or paper targets, cheaper RN or FMJs will do. Critical situations will call for purpose-built loads, capable of maximum effect. One thing to remember: There is no magic bullet. Properly designed projectiles play a key part, but bullet placement is crucial.

Many ammo makers publish charts showing the performance of their loads. The information may show the various calibers, MV, ME, trajectory, wind drift, and recommended sight-in ranges. They're worth a look, and will provide a basic understanding of trajectory.

To maximize our ammo choices, we can look toward firearms that aren't dependent on specific power levels for reliable function. A semi-automatic is fussy, but a pump action will eat just about anything. The same applies to a revolver – something we can file for further discussion.

The full line-up of metallic & shotshell choices (L-R): .22 LR, .357 Magnum, .308 Win., 12 Ga. birdshot, buckshot, and slugs. There's not much that couldn't be covered with these.

Chapter 7: The Gun Safe and Other Storage Methods

We'll look at some firearms in a moment, but first we'll need a proper place to store them. A common method – leaning a long-gun up against a corner wall – may have worked during a time when a firearm was viewed as just another household tool. Kids grew up around guns and nobody had locks on their doors. Times have changed. In our urbanized environment, firearms are increasingly a novelty. Many kids grow up in single parent households without father figures who fish or hunt. Even those children familiar with firearms will likely have friends with little-to-no experience, other than what they see on television. You can bet their viewing experiences probably won't include The Sportsman Channel, either.

One of our employees stopped in the office to explore handgun storage options. He kept a loaded double-action revolver hidden in a bedroom drawer. Believing in Murphy's Law, he unloaded it shortly before some visitors arrived. An hour later, everyone was stunned to see a four year-old walking down the hall with a K-frame Smith & Wesson. It was a sobering experience for all parties. So much for "hiding" the gun. We had a few solutions.

PORTABLE SECURITY

Not everyone may need a full-sized safe, but the means to deny unauthorized access is every gun owner's responsibility. In fact, California's laws make it a legal requirement. However, a completely fool-proof system is difficult to achieve. On top of that, we need to balance ready access against adequate security, within the limits dictated by expense.

Gun boxes. This topic came up during an NRA Instructor course. We were exploring various home storage options for 100 officers who had been issued semi-auto pistols. The NRA Regional Coordinator was a former police officer and showed us his personal solution. He bought a Gun Vault MV-500 lockbox with sequential keypad access. It runs on a 9-volt battery, but also has a security key override feature. The unit comes with a hardened cable that can be looped around a hard point object. The four keys are large enough to manipulate by feel, and the combination sequence can be programmed by the user. His was cabled to a bed frame. He opened it at night. He just closed the lid with his foot the next morning and slid it under his bed. His box was still going strong after three years of daily use. We subsequently purchased 120 units and most are in the field. At around $100, they're an affordable deterrent to unauthorized firearm access. The operative word is "deterrent." At some point, a determined individual with a pry bar will either gain access, or lug the whole thing off.

Gun Vault MV 500 with programmable touch pads & key override.

<u>Trigger locks.</u> They're another deterrent-type solution. Several years ago we were hosting a field school for a major firearms manufacturer. Their instructor opened a handgun case and produced a pistol with a trigger lock. He soon realized the key was elsewhere. He asked for a screwdriver and then popped the lock in half within seconds. We found the experience to be one of the more memorable moments in the program.

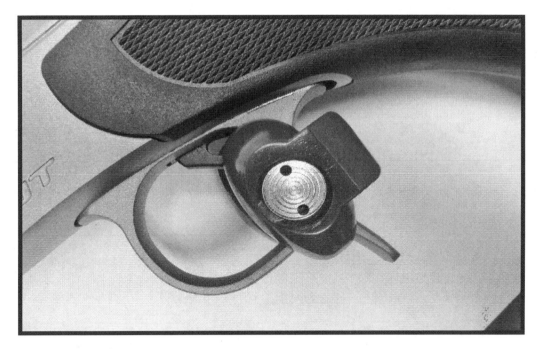

A gun manufacturer-supplied trigger lock – not too inspiring!

Cable locks. A coated, hardened wire is looped through the action of a firearm to interfere with its function. If enough play remains, the cable may be secured to a hard point as well. We actually prefer them to trigger locks. On most firearms you can find a spot to pass the cable through. It could be a magazine well, receiver bridge, or revolver top strap.

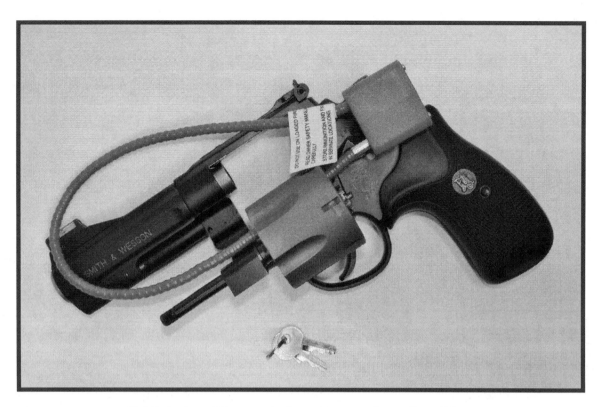

Cable lock, with room to loop it around another object.

Jury rigged solutions. On a revolver, even a padlock will work. So will a set of handcuffs, with one bracelet through the cylinder opening, and the other locked to some immoveable object. The same technique works with some shoulder-fired weapons, including many pump shotguns. Long-shanked padlocks will sometimes fit through action parts, too. Many firearms can be disassembled, permitting disabling of the gun. A bolt action rifle is a good example. On most designs, the bolt can be easily removed and secured in a smaller container. The same is true for an AR-15 bolt-carrier and bolt assembly.

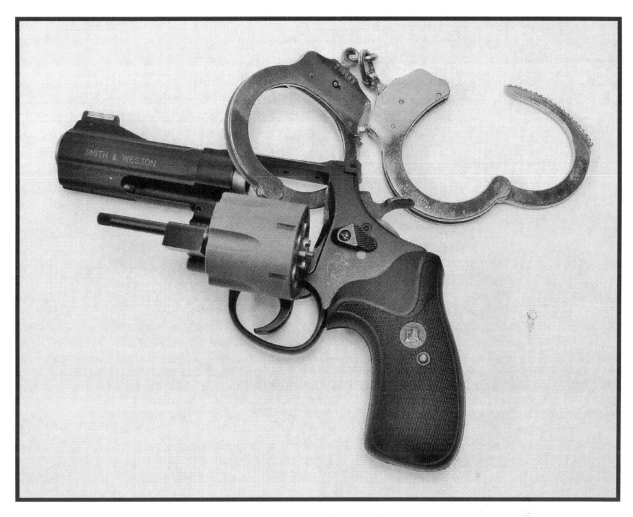

An old cop trick, but a long-shanked padlock is another option.

GUN SAFES

The best bet is a gun safe. You'll pretty much get what you pay for. Some are really only storage cabinets. The low-priced units may protect your firearms from kids, but they won't stop a thief. The best protection will involve two factors: weight and cost. I consider my safe more than just a way to secure guns. It's also a storage module that puts many key accessories in one convenient spot. Anyone who has ever fished around the nether regions of a closet full of debris will appreciate this feature. Mine is a basic box, but some have more elaborate features like contoured exteriors and revolving racks. The latter feature can even be purchased separately, for custom installation. Being a basic meat and potatoes guy, I just put the long guns most likely to see regular use up front. Before deer season, the back row gets switched with the varmint and target guns. Most people have seasonal clothes. I have seasonal guns.

Gun Safes

Plan for expansion. Choose a bigger safe than you think you'll need. Better to have a bit of extra room than wind up damaging your firearms while cramming them in. You'll want adequate height and width. Some firearms (like shotguns) are fairly long. A top shelf is really handy and these two factors dictate a height of around 60 inches. Mine is 30 inches wide. I converted a portion of one side to storage cubbies, losing a few gun slots as a result. The shelves are handy for scopes, knives, accessories, external hard drives for backed-up computer files, or most anything else of value. If the need arises later, it won't be much trouble to take them out.

It seemed plenty big when purchased!

I rigged two pegboard panels to the safe door. Large S-hooks permit storage of larger handguns, holsters, and equipment. I forced clear plastic tubing over their exposed metal shanks for protection from marring. Just about every square inch is occupied, which puts plenty of weight on the door. The hinges are plenty strong, but balance is a concern. While the safe's contents offset the door's weight to some degree, it really should be bolted to the floor. Many safes come pre-drilled. An older and smaller one I owned didn't, but I was able to drill four holes through its bottom.

Location. Planning will be necessary for convenient access, plus structural integrity. The bolts will need to bite into something solid, which can't be defeated from underneath. On top of that, a good safe and its contents will be heavy, requiring adequate support. In fact, the safe alone may present a serious installation challenge. If so, that's actually a good thing. If it's hard to get in the house, it'll be hard to remove. Before you purchase a safe, identify its final location. Then measure all of the stairways, halls, and door openings. I needed to remove two doors from their hinges, and the safe barely squeaked through at that. Prior to delivery, I also reinforced a set of exterior steps, and moved a kitchen appliance.

I bought my safe from a gun shop, but hired a local lock & safe company to move it. Believe me, it was money well spent! The cost was actually fairly reasonable and their stair climbing, powered dolly made short work of a few crucial steps. Nothing (including me) was bent, folded, or mutilated, and the whole process took less than an hour.

You'll need a place for your safe that has low humidity and a fairly constant temperature. Otherwise, condensation will ruin everything in it. De-humidifying devices are available, but won't offset extreme conditions. Look for a wiring provision since these units need power. Some safes actually come with integral systems, ready to plug in.

Protection and ratings. Gravitating toward serviceable but basic designs, I opted for a mechanical key & dial-combination lock. It's slower to open, but immune from electrical problems. Leaning toward simplicity, I went with a pebble gray finish instead of a high gloss tone. The money went toward construction over style. Others may go for a keypad. The latest technology involves an EMP-proof system. Some of the higher-end safes are true works of art with beautiful exterior paint.

Note the fire rating. Some last 2 hours. You get what you pay for.

When shopping for a safe, look for an Underwriters Laboratory Residential Security Container rating. Fire protection is equally important. You can find UL ratings for both security and fireproofing, which normally correspond to pricing. The process is fairly involved, but information is available online. Do some research before you buy. You'll generally get what you pay for, with increased cost resulting from better locks, thicker material, and improved fire resistance. Surprisingly, the "fireproofing" in many safes is actually sheetrock. During a bad fire, parts of a structure may collapse around the safe. If it's located above a basement, the floor may let go. A sealing gasket around the door is essential. It should expand when heated, which also helps keep out smoke and water. Either external or internal hinge designs will work. It might seem that an internal system would offer better security, but the door of a properly designed safe will remain fully secured, even if its hinges are completely removed. Many amateur burglars will spend extra time attacking the hinges instead of focusing on the locking system

You can help secure your safe by locating it out of plain sight. Some folks hide them in closets, or behind false walls. If it's secured in a corner, two sides will be more difficult to tamper with. Others build an actual vault with concrete walls and safe-type doors manufactured for just this purpose. If the safe is located in an area where water can accumulate, an elevated pad is a good idea.

Obviously, a truly theft- and fireproof safe will be very expensive. The mid-priced units aren't cheap either, and will set you back more than a grand. The cheaper models are more like cabinets. Buy the best safe you can afford and plan on it becoming an immoveable object. If you need to bug out, the safe will need to stay behind.

MOBILE STORAGE

Some interesting firearm security products are offered for vehicles. Small, handgun storage units like our Gun Vault boxes can be fastened to a trunk. Other long gun products mount in pickup beds, serving as surrogate liners for use with truck caps. Overhead units are available, too. Their main virtue is concealment, although they do afford a reasonable level of security. I'm no fan of long-term vehicular storage. Several friends come to mind that had firearms stolen from personal vehicles. The elements are another concern; not only humidity, but also temperature extremes.

For those who travel with handguns, portable gun boxes make sense. Those with a cable loop can be secured in a vehicle, but unhooked for use elsewhere. The big thing is to remember you have it. I know a few people who left handguns behind in hotel rooms.

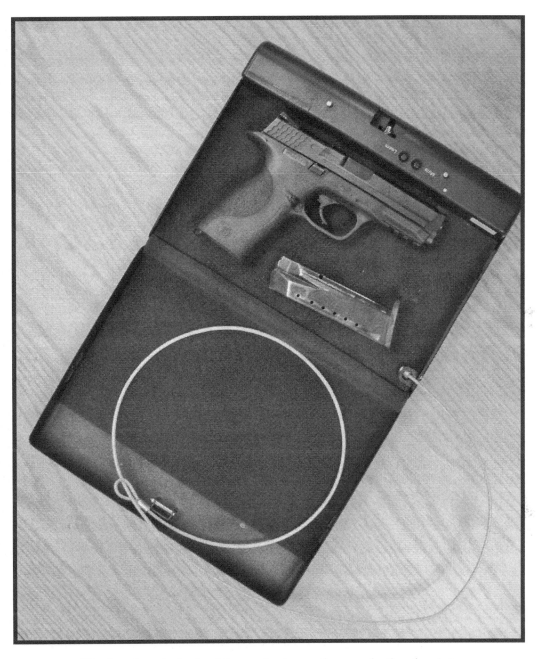

The hardened steel cable can be looped around a hard point.

Those transporting rifles or shotguns over long distances will want a hard shell locking case. For anyone flying, the extra expense for a rugged, airline-approved container is well-justified. In fact, some surface travel can be equally hard on a gun. Off-road driving can really jostle a rifle, knocking a scope out of zero, or worse. Even upon arrival, back country living can be tough on equipment. I was lucky to have a durable case the day a guide backed over my two-gun case with his pickup truck.

Soft cases are okay for local transportation, where legal. When passing through states like Massachusetts though, you risk losing your guns – or worse. As a resident of a saner locale, I generally use soft cases for home turf adventures. They take up less room and some even float. On an ATV, a hard shell gun boot is a safer bet. The firearm is protected from branches, rain, snow, or flying mud. One thing I really don't like is a horizontal rack. If you're serious about firearms safety (and you are, right?), you will religiously observe Rule #2 at all times. Your muzzle will at no time sweep someone, which puts the kibosh on horizontal vehicle mounts. For a real education in sloppy gun handling, back up and watch two people while they stow their rifles in a window rack. The same concerns apply to horizontal ATV rack mounts.

While cases are handy, they are ill-advised for long-term storage. The interior linings can hold condensation, which can quickly lead to rust. The same thing applies to storage in closets or drawers, where prolonged contact of clothing on steel can make a mess. I learned this lesson the hard way on a pretty, blued S&W revolver that was stuffed in a dresser drawer for less than two weeks. It was summer, with a period of fairly high humidity. Instead of surface rust, two inches of pitting resulted. It was a sickening sight!

OTHER STORAGE METHODS

Some people go to the extreme of actually burying guns. There are a few containers on the market built specifically for this purpose. I don't have any firsthand experience with them, but many moons ago we recovered enemy weapons that were similarly stashed. They were not only carefully wrapped, but also completely coated with heavy Cosmoline rust preventatives. Although that seemed to work most of the time, it was a real bear to clean off. The latest products are durable synthetic tubes with waterproof lids. MTM's smaller "Survival Burial Vault" costs only $20, and will accept a handgun, plus some extras. The larger 48-inch "Mono Vault Burial Tube" can handle long-guns, but costs more than $150. Inside the tubes, desiccant and specially designed plastic weapon storage bags are recommended.

Sometimes it may be expedient to just hide a gun in plain sight. A few clever products include wall-mounted clocks with swing-out faces that reveal a handgun storage compartment. You can even buy a hollowed-out book, which works much the same way.

Rubber coated magnetic handgun mounts can be attached to unobtrusive locations. They can be snapped onto metal cabinets, screwed to closet walls, or mounted to the undersides of desks or beds. Before going this route, it's worth thinking about access from a toddler's level.

Other options include wall-mounted pistol safes, which fit flush and anchor to 16-inch spaced wall studs. There are narrow, safe-type lockers which provide vertical or horizontal storage. They are often designed to accommodate one or two shoulder-fired weapons, which can be tucked within an unobtrusive location. American Security sells a Defense Vault, which will fit beneath a bed. Its angled and illuminated keypad can be activated at arm's length. Several vertical closet units work similarly, and are available from various manufacturers.

Plenty of options exist to meet nearly any storage requirement and budget. When quick access is a priority, a fumble-proof locking system will be needed; that works day or night. That eliminates the need for a key. Two other options include biometric locks, or sequential keypads. I don't have any first-hand experience with the biometric systems. They sound good in principle, the concept being that the lock actually "reads" your fingerprints. You might want to do plenty of research before buying one. Some of the comments I've seen concerning reliability have been mixed. So far, our keypad units have been working well. Practice is advised, from the most likely position it would be accessed from, in low light.

SUMMARY

A final benefit afforded by secure storage is peace of mind. With a bit of homework, you should be able to find something that will meet your needs. For purposes of this book we'll be filling a gun safe. Regardless of its size, with a safe at hand, we'll need a starting point. How do we buy a gun?

Chapter 8: Buying a Gun

A number of factors enter into the responsibilities of firearm ownership. We face federal or state statutes, some municipal restrictions, and the actual purchase process. Fortunately, our information age makes it fairly easy to access most of the legal requirements. A few great sources include The Bureau of Alcohol, Firearms, Tobacco & Explosives (ATF); the National Shooting Sports Foundation (NSSF); and the National Rifle Association (NRA).

Regardless of experience, all firearms owners should reserve some time to peruse the websites. They contain detailed information about federal and state laws, plus other useful links. Just a few key pieces will be high-lighted here.

FEDERAL REQUIREMENTS

The ATF is the primary agency responsible for enforcement of federal firearms laws. You can access their in-depth regulations, or reference a FAQ synopsis. Other links will get you into the various state laws and ordinances.

The 1968 Federal Gun Control Act. Under this legislation, we can't just order a firearm as we would a set of boots. Any retail transaction will need to go through a Federal Firearms License (FFL) holder. Likewise, we can't ship firearms across state lines from one citizen to the next. Private sales within the same state are generally legal, but an FFL holder will be needed for out-of-state transactions. Those purchasing rifles or shotguns must be 18 years old, and handgun buyers must be 21. These requirements are federal and some states have stiffer laws. The ATF doesn't regulate airguns, muzzle loaders or certain firearms classified as antiques. There are exceptions to these generalities, so time spent on the ATF's site is strongly advised.

Part of the NICS process: Form 4473.

The National Instant Criminal Background Check System (NICS). Any business you purchase a firearm from, whether a big-box store, your local hardware store, or a gun shop, will have a current FFL. You can't just slap some money down on the counter and walk out the door. Instead, you'll be handed a Form 4473, which you'll need to carefully read and complete. A number of questions (pertaining to criminal history, mental health background, residency, etc.) must be answered using check off boxes. Straw purchases are illegal and you'll need an ID. Your FFL holder will then phone the NICS hotline, which is run by the FBI. Hopefully, you'll be granted a "proceed." A "delay" means just that, with several possible outcomes. Again, the ATF site is your source for more information.

The National Firearms Act (NFA). Certain types of firearms and devices are more heavily regulated, including full-auto (machine guns), short barreled (SB) rifles or shotguns, and silencers (suppressors). However, legal ownership is possible through a lengthy federal process involving a special application, and issuance of a $200 stamp. A rifle with a barrel less than 16" or a shotgun barrel under 18" is illegal without a SB stamp. Some states impose further restrictions. Make sure you understand the legal aspects prior to proceeding.

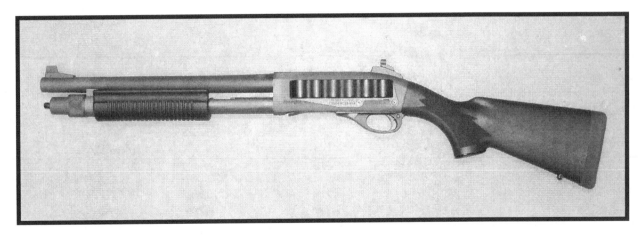

An NFA short-barreled (SB) shotgun – in this case a 14" Remington Model 870.

STATE & LOCAL RESTRICTIONS

The federal requirements apply to the entire United States by their very nature. Some states have more restrictive standards and a few have enacted draconian prohibitions. So-called "assault rifles" are a prime example, as are high-capacity magazines. Anyone purchasing a firearm through an FFL holder will likely be on safe ground, but private sales involving uninformed parties could easily incur problems.

__Permits and ID cards.__ Some jurisdictions heavily regulate private sales, requiring state-issued "Firearms ID Cards" or private-sale approvals.

Ironically, the number of states allowing individuals to carry a concealed handgun has recently increased. Most have a process involving an application, background check, some sort of competency requirement, and then issuance of a permit. Some states have reciprocity agreements which honor permits issued by other states.

Those states with "open carry" laws don't require permits for any firearms carried in plain view. I live in one, and can legally wear a handgun as long as it's not concealed. Although this is common practice among many sportsmen, I opted for a state-issued concealed weapons permit. Beyond personal protection, it's a safer bet if my coat ever covers the gun. It also provides a legal means to carry a loaded handgun in a vehicle.

Each state is different, so check the laws specific to yours.

__Hunting regulations.__ These can represent a third tier of restrictions beyond federal and state laws. For example, in my home state, ownership of a suppressor is legal, but hunting with one is not. Likewise, high-capacity magazines are a problem in our woods. A legal collection of 20 and 30-round AR-15 magazines needs to be exchanged for 5-shot versions before pursuing coyotes or other fair game. On a western prairie dog shoot, we legally burned through stacks of 20-round AR mags. Our biggest concern was the interstate drive and large assortment of firearms, ammo, and magazines.

LAWS PERTAINING TO HUNTING EQUIPMENT

GENERAL
Legal methods

Wild animals and wild birds may be hunted only by the use of firearms (not larger than 10-gauge), hand-held bow and arrow, crossbow or by falconry. Deer and moose decoys are legal; laser sights (red dots or beam) for firearms and bows are legal. Electronic calling devices are currently legal for deer, bear, turkey, moose, and coyote hunting. Electronic calling devices are illegal for migratory game birds.

Shotgun to be plugged

It is unlawful to hunt any migratory game bird with a shotgun originally capable of holding more than 3 shells unless the magazine has been cut off, altered, or plugged with a one-piece filler (incapable of removal without disassembling the gun), so as to reduce the capacity of the gun to not more than 3 shells in the magazine and chamber combined.

Illegal Methods

It is illegal to shoot an animal restrained in another person's trap without their permission.

Drawlocks and set bows are illegal unless otherwise permitted for disabled hunters.

Auto-loading firearm

(A firearm which reloads itself after each shot and requires a separate trigger pull for each shot.)

It is unlawful to hunt with or possess for hunting any auto-loading firearm which has a magazine capacity of more than 5 cartridges (plus 1 in the chamber for a total of 6), unless the magazine has been permanently altered to contain not more than 5 cartridges. (**Note:** This provision does not apply to .22 caliber rimfire guns or to auto-loading pistols with barrel lengths of less than 8 inches.)

Illegal use of lights

From September 1 to December 15, it is unlawful to use artificial lights from ½ hour after sunset until ½ hour before sunrise to illuminate, jack, locate, attempt to locate or show up wild animals or wild birds except raccoons which may be hunted at night with electric flashlights during the open season (see page 16 for details).

New This Year: An exception to this may be made for agents appointed by the Commissioner to hunt coyotes at night during this period under policies established by the Department.

Illegal ca...

Cartridges ...
bullets may ...

Deer hun...

No firearm ... caliber rimfir... firearms of an... deer with a bo... archery season... season on deer, ... a license that all... carry a handgun... deer or dispatch ...

Moose huntin...

It is illegal to use ... or shotguns using s...

Carrying conce...

A permit is required ... in Maine, except that ... trappers are exempt w...

A state hunting rule book. Note the auto-loading firearm limits.

Transportation and security. A few states have really onerous firearms restrictions (as does Canada). When traveling by vehicle throughout the U.S., we secure every firearm in a hard shell, locked case. Each is secreted in the most remote part of the vehicle. The trunk is best, followed by the rearmost portion of an SUV. We'll use a pickup bed, but only with an enclosed and locked cap. Everything gets covered up by clothes and gear. A trigger lock can offer additional security and is sometimes required. Manufacturers include them with new firearms.

Rigged up for interstate travel. The cases were later covered by other gear.

Some jurisdictions have more stringent transportation and storage requirements, so, once again, it pays to check.

HOW TO BUY A GUN

Let's assume you have a rough idea of what you're after. Perhaps you've done a bit of research and have an urge to shop. Do you head to some big box store or a local gun shop?

Big box stores. While the sticker price is important, there can be indirect costs. Staff knowledge can vary anywhere, but a full-line gun shop is your best bet for finding serious gun people. I have bought a few guns from the retail giants, but I knew *exactly* what I was after. Others who are less informed may have headaches. My son bought a popular .45 ACP pistol from a well-known national retailer for a fair, but not super-low price. The sales clerk then provided him with several boxes of .45 GAP ammunition; an entirely different cartridge unsafe to fire in a .45 ACP. We caught the problem, but he had a hassle returning it. The remedy also required a 150-mile round trip. He would've been better served by ordering it through our local shop. That said, the biggest retail chains have enormous buying power. Money talks and, at times, their retail prices can run well below the little guys. This can be especially true with ammunition.

<u>Gun shops.</u> We don't have any well-stocked gun shops in our immediate area, making hands-on decisions tough. For those more fortunate, a good, specialized gun emporium can serve as handy pro-shop. Like buying a car, it's often acceptable to haggle a bit on the sticker price. Once a deal is done, you may need accessories like scope rings or bases – items that can be difficult to select. The staff will probably know which combinations work best for your firearm, and will more than likely mount them for you. Do enough repeat business and they'll also cut you some slack if a problem does arise. Gun shops are also good sources for firearms training courses and gun club contacts. Some will even have their own range facility, complete with rental firearms.

A small shop, yes. But, personal attention doesn't hurt.

<u>The internet.</u> Yes, it is possible to purchase guns via the web, but I wouldn't recommend it for casual buyers. Here's how it works: You surf the net and locate a firearm on one of the popular

76

online classified gun sites (some of which are auctions). The seller will require advance payment and a copy of an FFL from someone in your state. Once both have been received, the gun will be shipped, but only to your FFL holder – usually a local gun shop – who will charge you a transfer fee. This additional expense is up to the store, but often runs $20 to $50. You'll normally incur a shipping cost as well, which may equal your transfer fee. The standard ATF Form 4473 and NICS process are still necessary. Some online vendors have a "no return" policy, while others offer a 3-day inspection period. Good photos help, and I always feel more comfortable dealing with a well-established online FFL dealer showing positive feedback.

Gun shows. They're fun and can present an opportunity to score on good accessory and ammunition deals. The tables are often staffed by area FFL holders, so a show provides a chance to sample the inventory from a number of shops, all under one roof. Most shows are crowded, meaning they're not an ideal spot for individualized attention. Furthermore, not every vendor maintains a brick & mortar storefront. This can present potential challenges if a future problem is encountered. Despite political theatrics, there really isn't a "gun show loophole." I've bought a few guns at shows and was *always* subject to the NICS process. More often than not though, I depart carrying only accessories.

Private sales. In my home state we have a well-known weekly swap & sell publication. One entire section is devoted entirely to firearms. A phone call and meeting can result in a legal sale between private parties, without any ATF paperwork or NICS process. A personal concern involves the background of the seller, and the history of the gun. I have bought a few interesting and more specialized firearms, but I generally avoid this route. As a private seller, I tend to avoid contact with strangers. Good friends or strong acquaintances are a different matter. Once more, although legal in my state, this method may not be in yours.

Record keeping. It's not a bad idea to maintain a file on every personal firearm. You can create a simple form containing a description of the gun, its serial number, purchase details, and disposition. In the event it is stolen or some other problem surfaces, you'll have some pertinent information to fall back on.

New or used? Good question! I'm not averse to buying a used gun after a careful examination. Sometimes the savings can be substantial. I've never been totally burned, but I have had a few surprises. Some were mechanical, while others boiled down to poor accuracy. A match-grade varmint rifle could have an eroded throat or sub-standard barrel, explaining its presence in the "used" rack. You may have no real way to know, short of actual live fire testing. A new barrel isn't cheap and replacement would drive the total cost beyond new retail pricing. A new gun is a safer bet, and may come with a guarantee. In fact, most of the major firearms manufacturers really stand behind their products. One thing to keep in mind: like a car, the moment you drive it off the lot, it's used.

Trades. Some of the big box dealers don't accept any firearm trade-ins, although they're the bastion of many gun shops. However, you can't expect full retail value. Any firearm you bring in will be, for all intents and purposes, "used." As such, depreciation needs to be factored in. Don't be surprised if you are only offered 60% of its retail value. The dealer needs a profit margin to pay the rent, cover payroll, and keep the lights on; not to mention insurance and taxes. Once in a while you may find a great offer on a more desirable firearm, and you'll normally fare better on a trade than you will on an outright sale.

Summary. For newer shooters, a full-line gun shop may be the best bet. You'll receive personalized attention while developing a future relationship for further needs. The markup on firearms is less than on accessories, where many retailers make much of their profits. You may decide to mail-order some incidental items. In fact, airguns and muzzle loaders can be bought this way, subject to any local restrictions. It pays to do some homework first, paying attention to your legal obligations.

Chapter 9: Filling the Safe: Essential Firearms

There are many types of firearms to choose from. Among the many shoulder-fired designs, most will fall under four general categories: bolt actions, lever actions, semi-automatics, and slide actions (pump). As we've discussed, a series of firearms that share common features can be beneficial. In that case, factoring in shotguns, a practical list is reduced to the last two types. Granted, there are break-barrel single-shots, and double-barreled over & under or side-by-side shotguns; however, none hold more than two shots. In the context of survival, capacity is desirable, so our candidates narrow down to pumps or semi-autos.

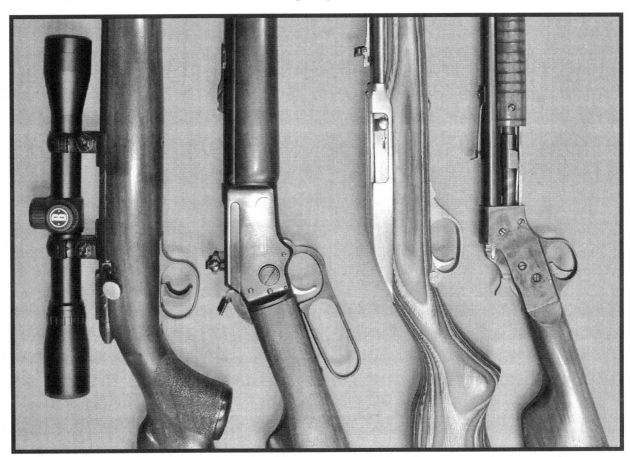

Bolt, lever, semi & pump action rifles – all in .22 rimfire chambering.

Economy factors in as well. The chart that follows is an example of a basic but practical firearms collection. At first glance, it may seem uninspiring, especially to us gun nuts. The firearms shown are plain Jane examples that won't dazzle onlookers. All are reasonably priced, and each has been chosen for a few special reasons:

Affordability. Don't forget - each firearm will require accessories such as scopes, holsters, etc. These add-ons constitute an overall "system", which may include cases, slings, and cleaning gear. We can't forget ammunition, and training may be necessary. Add everything up and sticker shock could bowl you over – especially if your base firearm cost is high.

Common function. To offset ammunition and training costs, how about considering a collection that shares similar operation? Remington's slide action models meet that requirement, providing a fairly standardized manual-of-arms. Whether using a shotgun or rifle, shooting one will reinforce skills for the other.

Ambidextrous operation. A higher-quality, sexy bolt action rifle is an enviable choice, but you will forfeit ambidextrous function. This is something to consider if any other users are left-handed.

Ammunition tolerance. By choosing the calibers that follow, you can capitalize on some very useful loads such as reduced-recoil and low-noise rounds. They won't cycle all semi-autos but, thanks to manual operation, pump guns and revolvers will eat them without problem.

Ease of maintenance. With a few basic tools, each firearm can be field stripped for routine servicing.

Legality. Here's something else to consider: *Every firearm on the list is legal in all 50 states!*

As a fringe benefit, none suffer from "assault rifle hysteria", a malady often associated with any type of black-finished firearm that is equipped with a pistol grip. Although these basic choices appear more benign, they can adequately defend the home front and put food on the table if your skills are up to speed. You could go for more exotic choices, spending lots more money, and still wind up jaded after the honeymoon ends. If money is tight, simple is good.

Example of a basic firearms battery: Approx. 2014 retail prices (actual costs may be vary)

Shotgun; 12 Ga: Remington M-870, slide action (shoots 2 ¾ & 3Magnum)........................ .$340*

Rifle; 22: Remington M-572, slide action (functions with lighter CB Caps, shorts & shot-loads) $550

Rifle; .308: Remington M-7600, slide action rifle (will function with light loads) $600*

Revolver; .357: S&W M-66, double action (also shoots lighter .38 Special loads) $650

* Buy with synthetic stock to improve weather resistance.

It's just an example. Right about now, I can see just about everyone with some firearms knowledge gnashing their teeth over the omission of their favorite brand, model, or caliber. First off, relax; there's a good chance you WILL see mention of it later on. Some firearms that come to mind (beyond the above-mentioned Glock, 1911, or AR-15) include Ruger's immortal .22 semi-automatic 10/22 rifle and Remington's centerfire M-700 bolt action. All are viable alternatives which will be covered thoroughly in other manuals in the PrepSmart© series.

It's nice to have firearms that share common function, but it's certainly not necessary. Many of us own guns that are like old friends. They're prized possessions if for no other reason than sentiment, and their owners generally know how to use them. Maybe the gun cabinet holds a Remington bolt action 22, received long ago as a treasured gift. It might include an older .30/30 Winchester Model 94 lever action handed down by a parent, or Grandpa's 12 gauge Ithaca Model 37 pump action shotgun.

To that end, first up is the gun that won the West, which wasn't a Colt Single-Action Army. Nor was it a Winchester lever gun. It was the shootin' iron most likely to be leaning in the corner of every sodbuster's dwelling.

THE FIRST GUN SAFE SLOT: A SHOTGUN

A common misconception is that you can just point a shotgun in the general direction of a target and make a hit. Not true! A shotgun is a smoothbore firearm, meaning the barrel doesn't have the spiral lands and grooves needed to stabilize a single projectile (an exception being purpose-built slug guns). You'll sometimes hear it called a "scattergun" in reference to its multiple projectile payloads. The pellets emerge in an expanding pattern which, at maximum ranges of 40-50 yards, may saturate several square feet; however, at room-length distances, a pattern may cover just several inches. Patterns are based on a number of factors ranging from gauges to chokes. We can also utilize single projectiles in a pinch to extend our range or tackle big game.

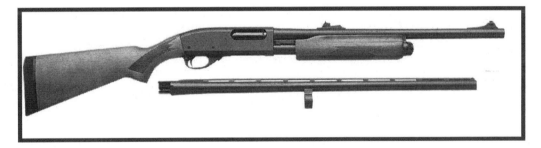

Remington Express M-870 with extra slug barrel.

Once understood, the shotgun affords some useful options, making it the first choice for our safe. A good starting point would be the Remington Model 870 12 gauge, slide action (or pump) shown in the chart. It's a straightforward, reliable design, well-proven during more than six decades of continuous production. Extra barrels are readily available to meet specific requirements. Starting with a basic Remington "Model 870 Express" equipped with a 26 – 28", 3" Magnum, ventilated rib bird barrel, one could later add a shorter, 21" slug barrel with iron sights to improve accuracy. Either could be swapped out in just a few seconds by unscrewing the magazine cap. It's like owning two guns.

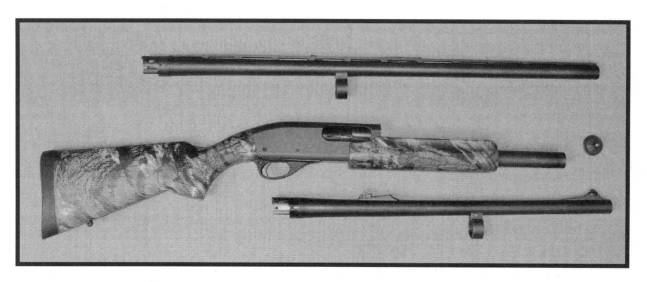

M-870: Swapping barrels is as easy as unscrewing the cap.

The Express bird barrels are threaded for Remington's interchangeable choke tubes, and come with a "modified" tube, good for 35-40 yards. A more open "improved cylinder" choke will throw wider shot patterns to help make hits at closer range. A "full" tube has more constriction to maintain the tightest spreads. Premium shot loads can be effective out to 50 yards if matched to that choke. The 3" Magnum loads come into play here, but for most other uses, lower-recoil 2 ¾" shells will do just fine.

M-870: IC, Mod & Full chokes. The "full" is in the barrel, but the wrench permits easy changes.

Slug barrels are available with smoothbore or rifled options. Each is primarily intended to fire a single projectile which, in its basic form, is a .73-caliber, 1oz. "bullet" that hits like Thor's hammer. Although the rifled version will be more accurate with some specialty slugs, the less expensive smoothbore is reasonably accurate out to 75 yards or more. It will also handle larger pellet buckshot loads that are good for defensive roles. Although 3" Magnum loads are offered, they kick like a mule. Premium 2 ¾" shells will more than suffice.

A basic Foster-type slug. It's a .73-caliber one-ounce bullet.

In basic bird barrel form, the gun is fairly manageable at around 7 ½ lbs. Remington offers many different 870 versions, including their "Super Mag", which can digest hard-kicking and extra-long 3 ½" Magnums popular with goose hunters. Fortunately, it will still feed 3" and lighter 2 ¾" shells.

12 Gauge shells: 3 ½″ Super Mag, 3″ Magnum & 2 ¾″ standard length.

The latest fad involves numerous add-ons, such as M-16 type stocks and extended magazines. Truthfully, there's nothing wrong with a factory-issue synthetic stock, which will preserve the handling dynamics needed for fast, instinctive shooting. While a few extra shells can be reassuring, a magazine extension kills the quick-change barrel feature. In basic form, the tubular magazine holds just four shells (plus one extra in the chamber); however, unlike most other repeating firearm systems, with practice it's possible to sustain capacity between shots.

Because its nuances are seldom understood, the shotgun manual that accompanies this series fully explores key information like shell types shot size, and chokes.

GUN SAFE SLOTS TWO AND THREE: A PAIR OF RIFLES

When accurate shot placement is necessary, or when distances are long, a single, well-placed projectile is necessary. The bullet must fly true to its intended path, and "rifling" imparts the necessary stability, spinning it much like a properly thrown football. Look in a rifle barrel and you'll see spiral "lands and grooves" cut to accomplish this purpose.

The choice of calibers is daunting, and one caliber alone won't cover every contingency. Those we select should be not only up to the job, but also widely available. Thankfully, with careful planning, we can assemble a modest rifle collection to harvest small game, or engage larger, distant targets. At a minimum, I'd reserve at least two slots in your safe for rifles.

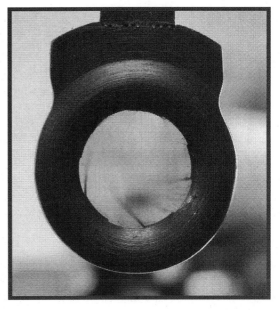

Slot two, a rimfire rifle. This very handy tool will permit quiet shooting for lower-cost practice, plus pest elimination and small game hunting.

Out of several rimfire choices, three are the most widespread: the venerable .22 Long Rifle; its more potent offspring, the .22 Winchester Magnum; plus the necked-down .17 Hornady Magnum. The stated attributes, plus widespread availability, make the .22 Long Rifle (LR) a great choice. With so many .22 rifles available, the real challenge involves choosing a finalist.

Rifling, seen through the business end.

Three popular high-velocity rimfires in .22LR, .22 WMR & .17 HMR.

Checking the chart again, you'll see a .22 LR Remington Model 572 "Fieldmaster" slide action. It comes from the same manufacturer as the other two shoulder-fired guns, and functions in a similar manner. It has a tubular magazine and, unlike many other rimfire rifles, will fire .22 Longs; .22 Shorts; and .22 CB Caps, in addition to .22 Long Rifles. The M-572 will thus handle everything from high-velocity rounds to some very quiet specialty loads.

.22 Short, Long & Long Rifle cartridges. The M-572 will feed them all.

The M-572 has iron sights similar to the centerfire M-7600; and its receiver is grooved for a scope. Accuracy is sufficient to harvest small game out to the practical limit of .22 rimfire ammunition; somewhere around 75 yards. The Model 572 can serve as a good "under-study gun", providing beneficial practice as well. The fire controls are similar to the pump action shotgun .308, but it's a bit trimmer, weighing 5 ½ lbs with a 21" barrel. Although cost is higher than many other models, the training quotient should not be ignored. Lower-cost practice can amortize much of the initial investment, and it's not dependent on specific types of .22 LR ammo.

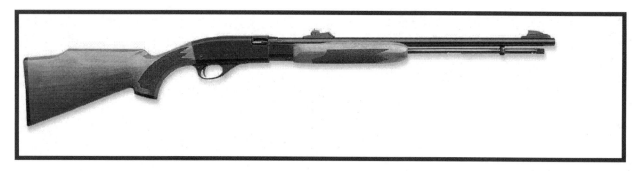

Remington Model 572 .22-caliber Fieldmaster pump.

For the complete lowdown on all things rimfire, check out the rimfire manual that accompanies this series.

Slot three, a centerfire rifle. Commonly referred to as a "high-powered rifle", here's the instrument you'll need for longer ranges and greater punch. The list of practical calibers is so long we'll need criteria to help narrow down the field.

The chart shows another Remington pump gun choice, in this case a .308 Model-7600. In military terms, this caliber is known as the 7.62x51mm NATO. Like the 12 Ga. and .22 LR, ammunition is widely distributed. The .308 Winchester has plenty of power and range, but recoil is bearable. In fact, low-recoil loads are now available that will roughly equal the power of a .30/30.

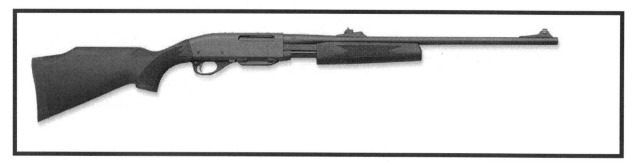

Remington Model 7600 .308 pump action rifle.

While the M-7600 isn't military-grade, it is fairly simple and reliable. It also has a detachable 4-shot magazine so extras can be carried. A higher-capacity after-market 10-shot version can transform the Remington to a makeshift "assault rifle." Remington capitalized on this concept by offering a Model 7600 law enforcement variant, but the simpler sporting version will work just fine. An inexpensive Weaver scope base will adapt the M-7600 to scope use via its drilled and tapped receiver.

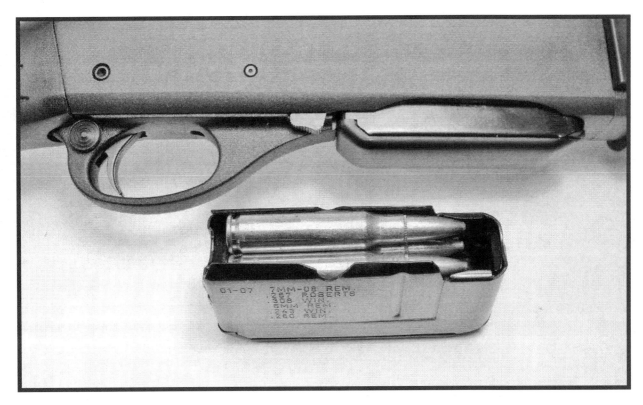

Remington standard safety location, and extra .308 magazine.

The synthetic stock version comes with a 22" barrel and weighs 7 ½ lbs. The slide release and safety function identically to the Model 870 shotgun. As such, shooter skills are transferable from one firearm to the next.

More detailed information is available in the centerfire rile manual that accompanies this series. There, you'll see coverage of semi-autos, lever actions, bolt guns, scopes, and ammunition.

Rationale. As previously mentioned, a slide action doesn't require ammunition of specific power levels for reliable function. Shooters can thus take advantage of specialty ammo, including low recoil shotgun and rifle rounds. The similar operation has value as well. The Remington pushbutton safeties are all located in the same spot, and can be reversed for left handed shooters. But, even without this switch, unlike a bolt action, you'll have a surprisingly ambidextrous firearm. Pumps are also cheaper than semi-autos and easier to clean. For those less disciplined, a pump is more tolerant of neglect. It will also run in bad weather, making it a dependable choice.

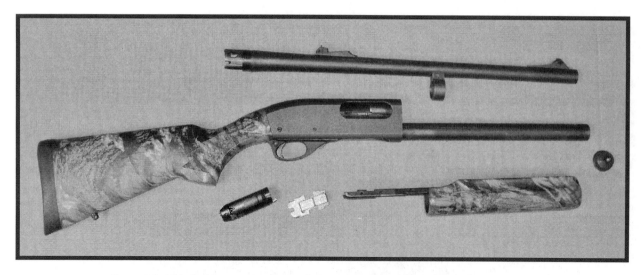

Rem M-870 field-stripped. Tool-less disassembly is quick and easy.

SLOT FOUR: A HANDGUN (or maybe, two)

Broad assortments of firearms fall into the handgun classification, which generally applies to non-shoulder-fired guns. Some are really more like hand-rifles, geared for high-powered cartridges and specialized situations. For our intents and purposes, we'll stick with portable options to facilitate hands-free and convenient carry. Two handgun types will meet our needs.

<u>Revolvers.</u> Here's an older design that many consider passé. A revolving cylinder contains multiple chambers, each individually aligned with the barrel. The first models were "single-action" (S/A) 6-shooter designs that required manual cocking of an external hammer prior to firing each shot. The western-style Colt .45 "Peacemaker" is a classic example. Firing, loading, and unloading are relatively slow (although today's cowboy action shooters can really make one roar). Cartridges are inserted individually through a swing-out loading gate. Ejection occurs through the same port, using a barrel-mounted rod.

Demand for a faster "double-action" (D/A) type resulted in a straightforward and reliable firearm that has served America's lawmen well for decades. For precise shooting, its hammer can be cocked to gain a short and light trigger pull. In dire circumstances, the gun may be fired by simply pulling the trigger. The longer, heavier pull self-cocks the hammer and cycles the action, permitting a fast defensive shot. As such, no "safety" is necessary. Pushing a thumb-latch permits the cylinder to swing outward for reloading.

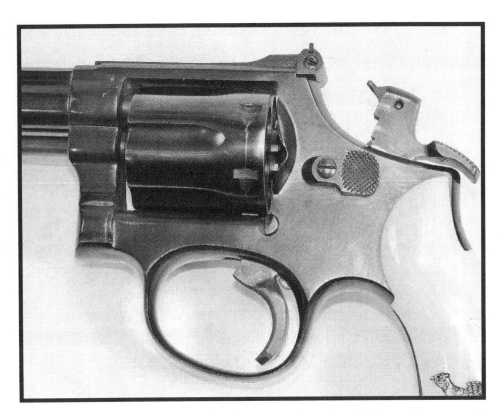

S&W D/A revolver, cocked in single-action (S/A) mode.

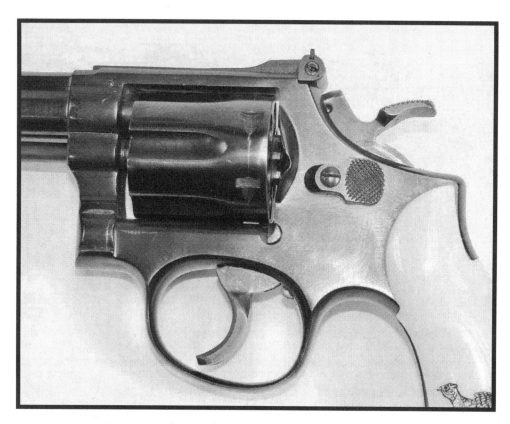

The same K-38 revolver, hammer down, in D/A mode.

S&W swing-out cylinder and thumb-piece latch.

Both types are still in widespread use by sportsmen, and the D/A revolver remains a popular choice among concealed-carry citizens. Capacity, at 5-8 rounds, is less than the newer high-capacity wonder guns, but simple can be good. In fact, the revolver is not only far from dead, but can be had in some very potent calibers. Balancing power against recoil, a .357 Magnum is hard to beat. The chart shows a 6-shot, double-action (D/A), Smith & Wesson (S&W) Model 66 with a 4" barrel. It's a mid-size offering that weighs around 36 ounces, and is made from stainless steel. Sights are adjustable to accommodate a variety of loads. Because the revolver's design doesn't rely on certain power levels to cycle the action, it is lighter-kicking and less expensive, .38 Special loads can be fired as well as full strength .357 Magnums.

S&W Model 66 .357 D/A stainless, 6-shot revolver.

Furthermore, a double-action revolver requires little effort to load and unload. Some people have trouble operating a semi-automatic due to heavy spring tension, a non-existent problem with a revolver. From a survivalist's perspective, it's a hard system to beat.

The Model 66 is a "K-Frame." Smaller 5-shot J-Frame S&Ws are available, which are easier to hide but a bit harder to shoot accurately. The Model 686 is an "L-Frame", and is a bit larger than a K-Frame, but can be had with a 7-shot cylinder. The big "N-Frame" can be had as an 8-shot variant. Balancing size against ease of shooting, the Model 66 or 686 are both great choices.

S&W M-60 .38 Special J-frame (B) & M-686 .357 L-frame.

Pistols. This classification generally applies to those handguns without a cylinder, non-revolvers. For our purposes, it will cover semi-automatics, which fire and cycle a new round each time the trigger is pulled. Many provide a large amount of rounds, at the expense of more complicated operation. Specific ammunition is needed to reliably power the action. In general, a heavy "slide" reciprocates to feed live rounds from a magazine housed in the grip. Upon discharge, the slide travels rearward, compressing a "recoil spring", while ejecting the spent cartridge case. It then surges forward under considerable spring tension, to strip the next cartridge from the magazine, and shove it into the chamber.

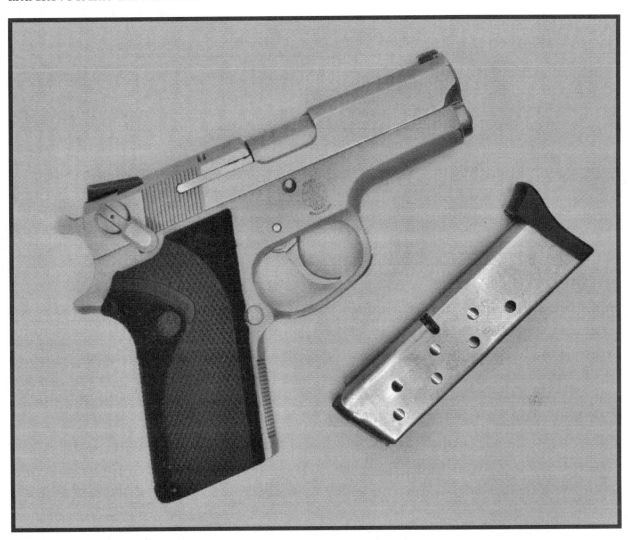

S&W M-3913 9mm D/A pistol: 1st shot can be fired S/A or D/A (similar to revolver).

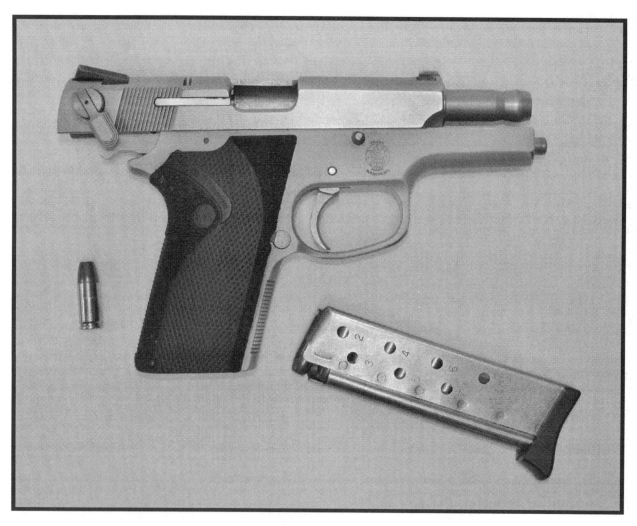

Slide locks open after last shot (shown with loaded magazine).

For our purposes, the minimum caliber should be 9mm, which offers manageable recoil and high capacity of up to 17 rounds, or more. The larger .40 S&W is another great choice, falling between the 9mm and venerable .45 ACP (Automatic Colt Pistol). Capacity will usually be around 15 rounds for full-size versions. For those that can manage its extra size and recoil, the immortal .45 ACP is a reassuring choice. Ammunition costs are commensurate with caliber sizes, with 9mm being the most easily found. Despite rumors to the contrary, it's a viable choice with today's defensive loads.

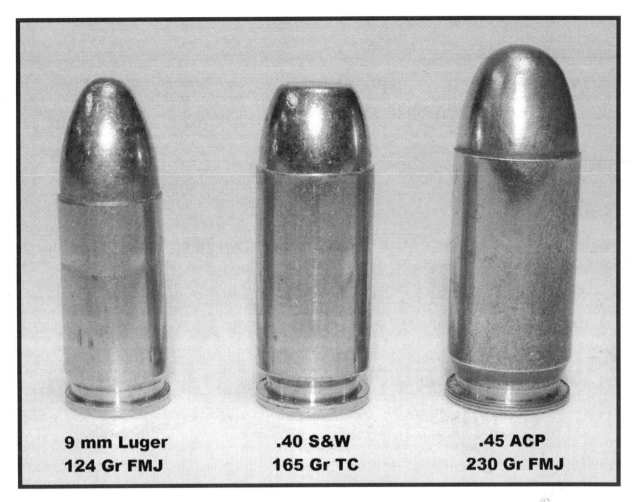

Three popular centerfire pistol rounds.

Dozens of pistol choices exist, making a final pick daunting. The latest genre, typified by Glock, has polymer frames and no external "safety." We've had great results with an inventory of 200 similar S&W "Military & Police" pistols in 9mm and .40 S&W calibers. Ours have a "magazine disconnect" that prevents discharge if the magazine is removed. While some professionals hate this feature, it can have value. Prior to disarming, you can remove the magazine but leave a round in the chamber. The pistol can then be secured in a tamper-proof location like a locking gun box.

S&W M&Ps: experience based on an adequate sampling.

An optional external safety variant is available, and the M&P comes in several sizes from 3.5" compact through 5" full-size. The smallest versions are pretty feisty in the larger calibers, although the 9mm is controllable. The service pistol mid-sized version with a 4.25" barrel is a good compromise, weighing 24 ounces. It has non-adjustable or "fixed sights", which are well-regulated from the factory. A "night sight" version is worthwhile, providing Tritium-powered elements that glow 24/7.

S&W M&Ps: 5" competition, 4 ¼ service" & 3 ½" compact models.

Ergonomics are outstanding thanks to interchangeable grip options. Maintenance is a breeze. Barrels and slides are stainless steel, coated with a durable, dark, non-reflective finish. Smith & Wesson offers a .40 "carry & range kit" package for those starting from scratch. You get a holster, magazine pouch, two extra magazines, and a few extra gadgets in one box. All of the major pistol brands will run reliably, so a good choice really depends on personal preference.

Which type? A revolver is simple to operate and ammunition-tolerant (working with ammo of varying power), but has limited capacity and is slower to reload. A pistol is more complicated and less ammunition-tolerant, but offers higher capacity and faster reloads. Either design may be a good choice, depending on your situation. I'd feel suitably armed with a revolver or a pistol, and I enjoy shooting both types.

An extra rimfire slot? A matching .22 caliber handgun offers many of the same advantages described in the rifle listing. S&W sells a few rimfire versions of their centerfire revolvers, as well as the M&P pistol. They're lots of fun to shoot, and provide a great practice tool.

Handgun rationale. It's part of the essentials listing because, if you seriously need one, you'll need it more desperately than anything you've ever needed before. It does no good to own one, but not have it available. Size, weight, recoil, comfort, and confidence all play a role. Clearly, these are personalized considerations which will dictate your choice. Save a spot in your safe for at least one such handgun, and possibly two. In fact, many will seek a third, smaller gun for deep-cover concealment. There are many facets to this subject, which are covered in the handgun manual that accompanies this series.

A ONE-GUN LOCKER

What if you only could have one gun? I'd hate to be in that position, but if it came down to this predicament, my choice would be a 12 Gauge Remington Model 870 shotgun. It would be a magnum receiver version capable of firing all loads up to 3". I'd fudge it a bit and outfit the gun with two barrels, knowing either could be quickly installed. My primary barrel would be a 26 – 28 inch bird barrel with interchangeable choke tubes. By simply unscrewing the magazine cap with my fingers, I could swap the bird barrel out for a shorter, 21 inch, rifle-sighted slug barrel. Viola, a shotgun and rifle rolled into a single firearm.

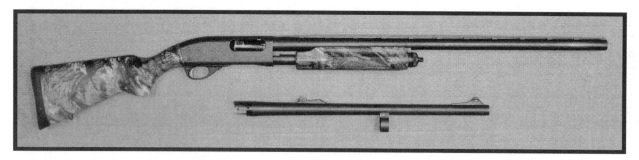

A two-barreled M-870 set: the do-all, one-gun solution.

SUMMARY

These choices are merely a few examples in a very crowded marketplace. For those either starting from scratch or having a more casual interest in firearms, it's a nuts & bolts list that may prove useful. Some people may already own some firearms, but want more in-depth information. Others may have interest in different firearms systems such as bolt actions, lever actions, or semi-autos. The manuals in this series are designed for these reasons. You can use them to pick and choose, creating a personalized inventory.

Chapter 10: Extra Slots for Other Systems

Beyond the essentials list, we may wish to add a few more handy choices. They could possibly be considered "specialty guns", although the iconic AR-15 has, in recent years, assumed a well-established and justifiable role among mainstream users.

The AR-15. In case you're wondering why none appeared in the "Essentials" list, the reasoning involves expense and ballistic performance. Prices are relatively high. The power and noise of the .223 (or 5.56mm NATO) is well in excess of any rimfire, but still inadequate-to-marginal for use on larger game. Some recent AR-15 chamberings have improved power, but availability of ammunition remains limited. The latest concern for some involves legality resulting from the rash of anti-gun hysteria.

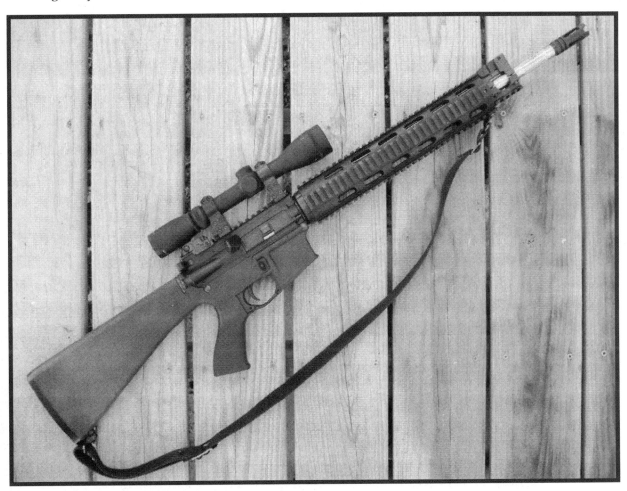

AR-15 with 18" barrel, Leupold 3x9 scope & back-up iron sights.

The *much* larger AR-10 can handle full-power cartridges like the .308 (or 7.62x51 NATO) but again, pricing knocks it off a basic list. Prior military folks, or others well-versed on the AR system, could assemble an alternate rifle battery consisting of three (or more) variants, all using the AR-style platform. These could include a .22 LR, .223/5.56mm, and .308/7.62x51 NATO. Because the AR-15 is the ultimate "transformer", more exotic chambering can be used by simply switching upper receivers. In many cases, merely disengaging two pushpins located in the lower receiver unit is all it takes to make a conversion.

Switch-top AR: .223 HB precision upper & mounted .300 Blackout.
One lower receiver provides two different rifles!

A good example is the new .300 Blackout, which can fire .30-caliber bullets from a modified .223 cartridge case. Although primarily designed to fire heavy subsonic bullets through a suppressor (silencer), lighter supersonic projectiles work well enough to take deer or hogs at 200 yards. The odds of finding .300 Blackout rounds at your local hardware store are slim, but it makes an interesting AR alternative. Since standard magazines work with either round, a conversion-upper is feasible.

Is there a widespread role for a system like the AR-15? You bet, but for now, we'll place it on the specialty list. For those considering one, check out the in-depth AR-15 manual that accompanies this series.

Backup or concealed-carry handguns. To keep a lid on costs, just one mid-sized revolver was shown on the basic firearms list. Depending on personal preference, it could have just as easily been a semi-auto pistol. Many people could conceal either type with the right clothing. Still, the demand for more compact handguns is understandable. Through careful planning, we could choose one with similar function to support familiarity. A little 5-shot S&W .38 Special J-Frame with a 2" barrel is extremely portable, and works identically to the 4" K-frame.

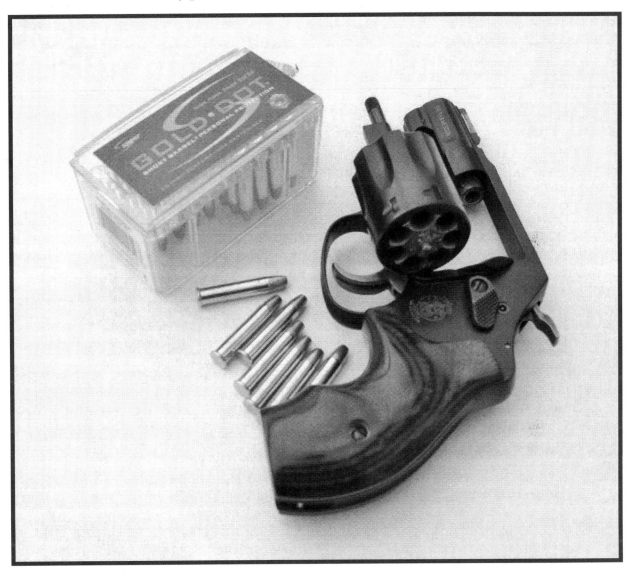

S&W J-frame. This one is a .22 Magnum, but it still works identically.

For pistol people, S&W sells the very compact 8-shot "Shield", which is very much like a shrunken M&P. It has a 3" barrel and a thinner grip sans interchangeable inserts. Options include 9mm or .40 S&W, with the latter being fairly stout to shoot on such a small pistol frame. After testing both, I went with the 9mm version. It feels very familiar and is surprisingly accurate. Although a small thumb safety is present, I don't use it, relying instead on the similar full-sized M&P features. For deep cover, S&W sells the even smaller .380 "Bodyguard", which was recently re-tooled to resemble their M&Ps.

S&W 9mm Shield – a compact but shootable carry pistol.

Small handguns are more difficult to shoot well. I always seek a balance of something small enough to hide, but big enough to support effective hits. The whole concealed carry concept has many issued to consider and you can learn more about them in the handgun manual that accompanies this series.

Precision rifles. I'm hesitant to use the term "sniper", which has many connotations. Still, many shooters are very interested in accurate long-range work. The tool for this trade is a heavy-barreled bolt action centerfire, capable of launching a flat-shooting bullet. It will typically have a large scope with high magnification, and be equipped with accessories like a folding bipod, rangefinder, and hard shell case. As often as not, the rifle will be a Remington Model 700 with a synthetic stock. The .308 Winchester is a starting point, with more potent calibers now in vogue.

Typical heavy-barreled precision bolt action,
in this case a Remington Compact Tactical Model 700.

The plain Remington M-7600 pump shown in the basic chart is perfectly adequate for most high-powered rifle use. It will launch 150-grain .308 bullets at around 2700 fps, while putting three shots inside 2" at 100 yards without human error. This translates to 8" groups at 400 yards, meaning every shot should strike within 4" of its intended path. Of course, the human factor will expand these groups, but that's still useable accuracy for most situations.

The longer-barreled precision bolt guns will typically be twice as accurate, and a shoot a bit faster. Their thick barrels are stiffer to help absorb heat, but weight will be substantial. As such, they are really a specialized firearm. For those inclined, a .308 may be a good pick due to ammo availability. Premium loads with heavier bullets can shoot a bit flatter and help buck the wind at longer ranges. In skilled hands, with the right equipment, predictable hits are possible out to 800 yards. For most of us, the practical range will be half that, which is still close to a quarter mile. This performance comes with a price and, considering its specialized role, shouldn't be a top priority.

Combination guns. I'm a sucker when it comes to dual-purpose, two-barreled shotgun/rifle firearms. They are a break action, over & under (O&U) design which may have an exposed or internal hammer. The shooter chooses which barrel will fire by use of a small selector lever. Logic might dictate that two guns could be rolled into one useful package, capable of covering just about all bases. Unfortunately, personal experience indicates otherwise. The reality is that you'll actually be carrying two single-shot guns, which may not be the end of the world, but is a limiting factor nonetheless. With plenty of practice, a user could become adept at switching between barrels for a fast second shot.

I own a European 12 Ga./.223 that has seen intermittent use for more than three decades, but truthfully, despite considerable firearms experience, I remain an amateur user. More than once I've lined up on some distant quarry and carefully squeezed off a shotgun shell instead of a bullet. It's somewhat humbling and actually dangerous if the reverse occurs on a sky lit target. Still, such firearms can be useful, which explains their popularity in Europe.

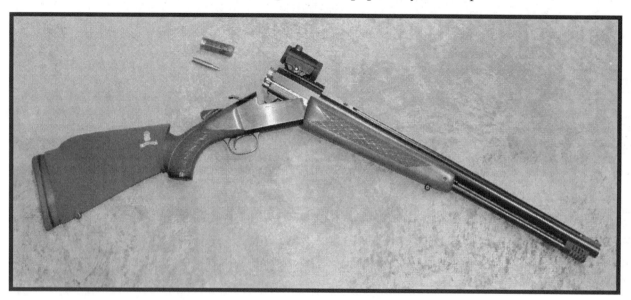

The author's veteran Tikka .223/12 Ga. combination gun, no longer in production.
Fortunately, other good choices remain.

A line of Russian-built "Baikal" combination guns has been intermittently marketed by several vendors. It can be had in several interesting caliber and gauge selections, including O&U rifle barrels. For decades, Savage sold their Model 24, which is most commonly encountered in .22 rimfire & .410 or 20-gauge variants, along with other choices. It finally disappeared, but has been replaced by a new and modestly-priced Model 42 synthetic -stocked .22 LR (or .22 Magnum) over .410 shotgun.

Such guns may at times be useful in secondary, survival roles. They can be disassembled for compact stowage in a backpack, vehicle, or aircraft. When used for these purposes, a fairly basic gun would be the better bet.

Single-shots. Most comments here will pertain to shotguns or centerfire rifles, which will fall in the specialty listing for the reasons above. Believe me, you can spend serious money on a single-shot rifle for a graceful and elegant example of the gun-making art. With deeper pockets, I'd spring $5,000 for a Blaser K-5 in a minute.

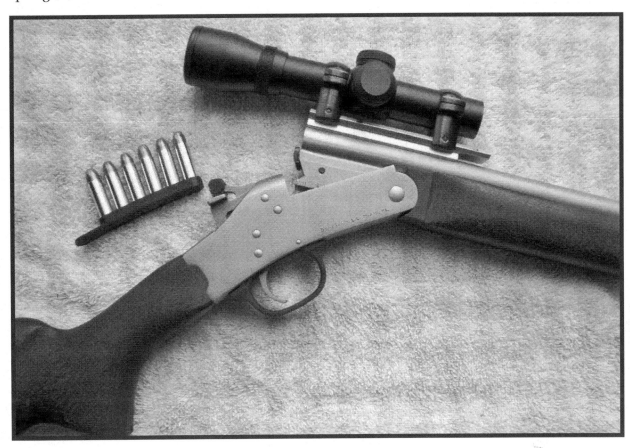

A poor man's stalking rifle, a single-shot Rossi .357 Magnum. It shoots .38 Specials, too!

Meanwhile, I own a beater .357 Magnum Rossi rifle, which set me back less than $150 brand new. Although it doesn't see a whole lot of regular use, unlike my combination-gun, I don't struggle with it. Economy, simplicity and fast takedown make it a very useful addition. H&R and NEF sell similar, basic single-shot rifles and shotguns, including survival-oriented models, and rifle/shotgun barrel sets. CVA sells an affordable "Scout", and a pricier "Apex" model that offers interchangeable barrels.

More single shots: These stainless CVAs have .300 Blackout barrels.
The Scout's (B) is dedicated, but .50 Muzzle-loading & .308 barrels interchange on the Apex.

Thompson Center really popularized the concept of pre-fitted barrels, offering single-shot pistols as well as rifles. Both types shared the same frame and the line continues with today's "Encore", an extremely versatile switch-barrel design. Rossi came out with an affordable switch-barrel line – the "Wizard." Both CVA models and the T/C are available in stainless.

I wouldn't choose a single-shot as part of a core firearms battery, but might consider one for ancillary use. Most can be easily disassembled for discreet storage. The more basic models are very affordable, which is why I use one as a "truck gun."

Airguns. Out of every gun-type listed here, these will really be the most specialized. Not everyone will need or want an air-powered system, some of which are dependent upon CO_2. Many more employ a spring-driven piston to generate a blast of air. Pump-up pneumatics rely on a succession of pressure strokes to charge an air reservoir. A higher-end pre-compressed pneumatic (PCP) variation employs a reservoir of high-pressure air which may be charged from a scuba tank or special pump.

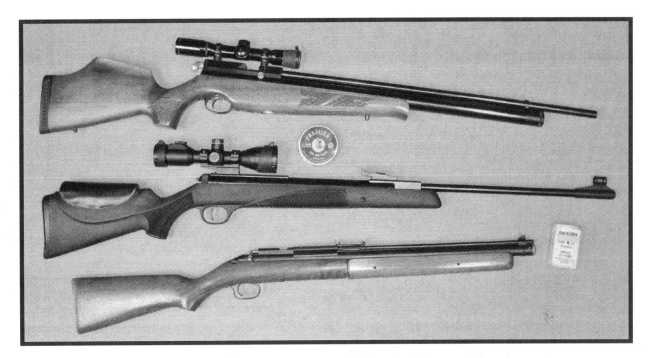

Three different airgun types: Air Arms .22 PCP (T),
RWS .22 P-34 springer (c),old Sheridan 5mm pump-up pellet gun (B).

Performance and pricing varies widely, from the simplest BB guns to some incredible examples of precise manufacturing. Most airguns are relatively quiet, which can be a major advantage if stealth is called for. My favorite .22 PCP rifle isn't really any louder than a staple gun, but has tipped over crows beyond 90 yards. A few such guns are available in head-turning calibers like .45, or even .50-caliber. A PCP gun is my preferred choice, but it is dependent on some sort of external air supply. The pump-up pneumatics are self-contained, but fairly loud, and tiring to shoot. Spring-powered guns are typically cocked by a hinged barrel, connected to its piston by a linkage. Others use an under-lever, or side-lever arm. In some cases, the "spring" is actually a gas-ram design similar to some shock absorbers. Due to recoil dynamics, the "springers" are more difficult to shoot consistently. On the other hand, useable power can be had in an entirely self-sufficient platform.

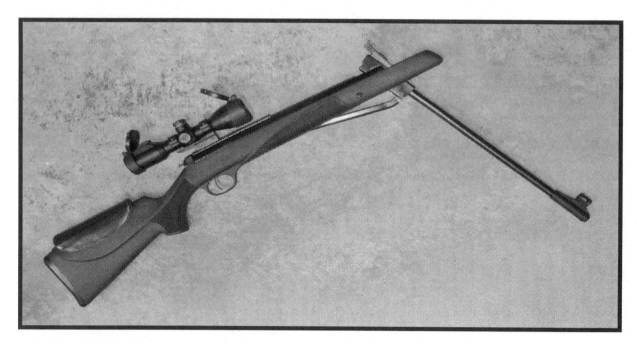

RWS P-34 Springer in cocked position.
A single stroke compresses its powerful spring-driven piston.

The most common caliber is .177, which fires a wasp-waisted pellet that loosely resembles a badminton birdie. Muzzle velocity can exceed 1000 fps, approaching .22 LR speeds, although mass is considerably less (25%). The next most popular airgun pellet is a .22 caliber version. Either is fairly common, and the slightly bigger .22 is a better hunting choice. Either pellet could be lethal to humans, but neither has the power or range of a .22 rimfire. For this reason, their use should be limited to smaller game like squirrels.

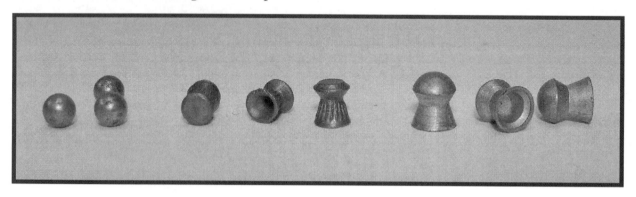

An airgun projectile sampler: BBs (L), .177 pellets (C), .22 pellets (R).

Airguns are not regulated by BATF and, from a federal point-of-view, have non-firearm status. They can be purchased by mail order, subject to any local restrictions.

We'll take a closer look at the specialty firearms in their respective manuals. Meanwhile, we'll need some gear.

Chapter 11: Accessories and Equipment

Referring back to the "basic firearms" chart, you can see a few examples listed, but no specific accessories. We need wiggle room in our budget for some necessary items, and the list may be a bit longer than expected.

RIFLE & SHOTGUN ACCESSORIES

While it's true that both of the rifles shown in the chart come with open sights, each would greatly benefit from a better aiming device. Most of today's high-powered rifles are designed to accept a telescopic sight, more commonly referred to as a scope. A decent one is a sizeable investment, which may equal the cost of a rifle. Slings, carry-cases, and cleaning kits are other key pieces. Since these items really drive up the overall cost, they need to be chosen carefully.

Scopes. With so many brands, magnifications, and features available, how do we make the right choice? It's probably safe to say that many shooters really sell themselves short in this area. A common mistake includes buying a bargain-basement model, which may result from failure to budget for the overall system. An extremely large scope, or one with too much magnification, is another pitfall to avoid. Eye-relief (the distance from your eye to the rear lens where the image is visible) is a major concern. The wrong combinations can result in an unusable setup, or one difficult to mount. Some selections just won't work, while others can give you fits.

Even a .22 rifle deserves a decent scope. Today, there are several good choices that won't break the bank. Many are variable 3x9s, but a straight 4X will do just fine. When cost is an issue, your money can go toward the simpler fixed-power model, rather than one with more moving parts. I'd trade the trick models with range-compensating features for sturdy but basic construction. Please buy a 1" tube instead of the junk 7/8" bargain-store types. You'll want to spend somewhere around $100, although a 4x Leupold is worth an extra C-note if you can swing it.

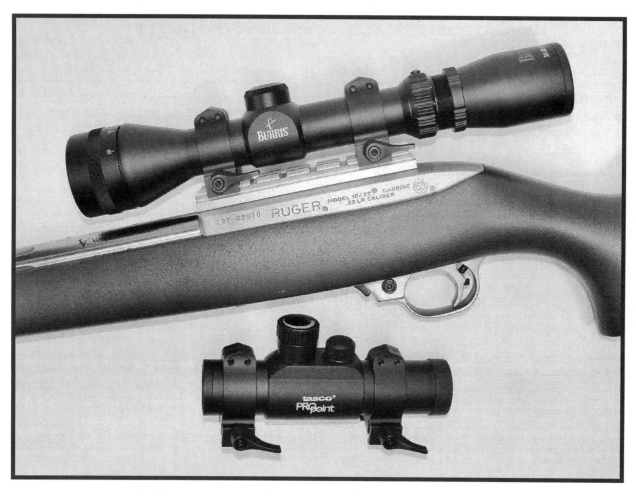

A rimfire 3x9 scope & electronic dot sight mounted in Warne QD rings.
A few twists of the levers permit use of either with no appreciable loss of zero.

The centerfire will likely see harder service, which could possibly involve a crisis. A dependable scope is essential and will cost a bit more. Since we're spending extra money, a quality variable-power 1x4 or 2x7 will serve you well. You'll gain plenty of mounting latitude and a compact package capable of meeting your needs. On the lowest settings, you'll have a large field-of-view so targets can quickly be located in the wider image. The higher settings can be used for more precise shooting, using the more restricted image. Among many viable choices, you can buy a decent Leupold, Redfield, or Nikon for under $250.

Tools of the trade: This Leupold 2x7 VX-2 has been through hell and back, but it keeps on going.

<u>**Scope mounts.**</u> The choices are nearly as mind-numbing as the number of scopes, and many are quite expensive. Because we started with basic firearms, we shouldn't need pricey, tactical types.

The .22 pump has a 3/8" grooved receiver that will accept "tip-off" rings. Built-in clamps can be tightened to secure the scope to the rifle. Rimfire scopes often come with such rings, but if not, they're fairly reasonable.

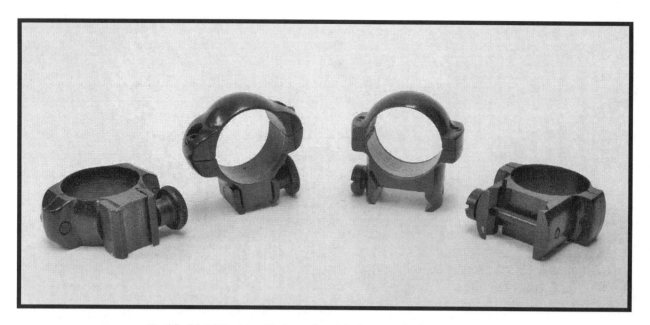

Redfield 3/8" tip-off rings for .22 dovetailed receivers (L),
and Burris Zee Rings for Weaver-type mounting (R).

The .308 is typical of most centerfire rifles, requiring two parts, a mounting base and separate rings. The base screws to the top of the rifle's receiver, using factory pre-drilled & tapped holes. Two separate rings are then cinched to the base in a manner similar to the rimfire. The "Weaver" types are perfectly adequate and affordable. Cost should be around $40. Avoid the cheapest rings, which are made from pot-metal. For a bit more, you can buy QD rings.

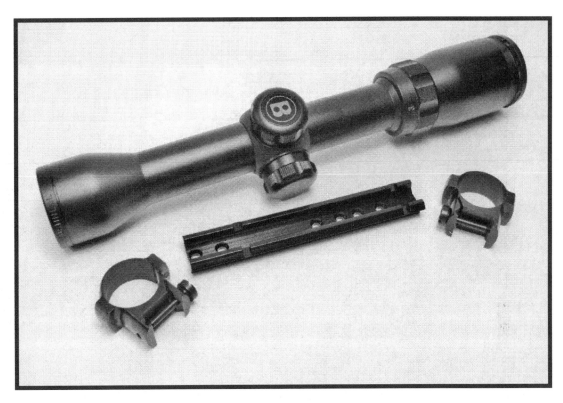

A basic system showing Bushnell Banner 1x4 scope, Burris low 1" Zee Rings, and Weaver base – inexpensive but strong mounts.

One thing I'd avoid is any type of "see through" mount. In theory, it makes sense, the idea being that you can still use the factory iron sights while peering through openings underneath the rings. The reality is that your head will come off the stock, degrading shooting form.

Shotgun choke tubes. The newer Remington Model 870s (along with many other models) are designed for interchangeable chokes. Short, threaded inserts of slightly different constrictions can thus be screwed into the muzzle-end of the barrel to regulate shot-pattern size. If you purchase a Remington Model 870 Express with a 26 or 28" bird barrel, it will probably come with just one tube, a "modified" choke. It will throw shot patterns effective out to approximately 35 yards. Beyond that distance the pattern will probably be too dispersed for predictable hits. At 25 yards or closer, the pattern will be so concentrated that hits on flying targets will be difficult. Game will also be shredded from a centered pattern. An extra "improved cylinder" tube will have less constriction to solve these problems. A "full" choke can be inserted for long-range shots of 45 -50 yards. The two extra chokes are a minor investment of $30 or less.

A set of Rem-Choke tubes, MTM case, and Remington's simple wrench.

Extra shotgun slug barrel. A shorter 21" smooth-bore barrel with rifle sights can fill two roles. It will fire bullet-like lead slugs with useable accuracy out to 75 yards, hitting like a sledgehammer. A switch to buckshot will provide a formidable defense tool. Switching barrels is as easy as simply unscrewing the magazine cap. The extra $150 cost is well worth it.

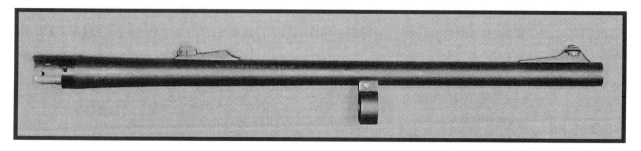

Extra Remington M-870 slug barrel with adjustable open sights.

Sling. I consider one essential. It frees your hands for use of binoculars, dragging game, or long-duration outings. With the right QD studs, you can quickly swap one sling between several firearms. You may need to install the studs, which typically come with swivels. A magazine cap unit is offered for the M-870 shotgun. A nylon sling is affordable and will dry quickly if wet. It's also lighter and quieter than leather. After threading each end through a swivel, you can depress the latches to attach them to the studs.

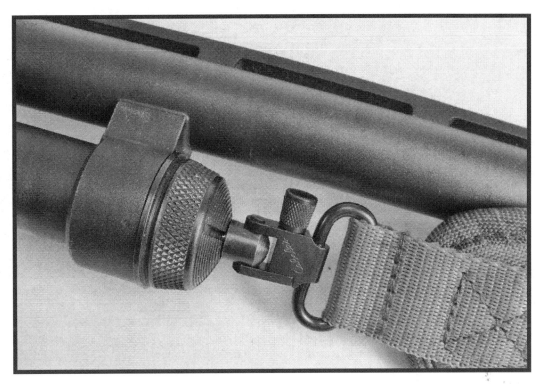

QD sling swivel with knurled screw-in safety detent, shown on M-870 magazine cap.

Soft case. For $20 you can own a padded carry case with a heavy-duty zipper closure. Some will even float. A case will prevent damage to your firearm during transportation in a vehicle or boat. Don't use it for long-term storage because humidity may cause rust.

Rem M-870 with some basic accessories.

Cleaning kit. Pre-packaged systems are one good way to get started. You'll get brushes, patches, solvents, and a cleaning rod. Later on, minor incidentals can be picked as needed. The rod will probably consist of threaded sections, which are harder on a rifle barrel than a one-piece unit. A pull-through cable system is another option that can be coiled up for compact storage. Still, a good one-piece rod is worth owning. Many kits come with a shotgun adapter, which accepts the larger brush threads. For regular use, a thicker-diameter shotgun rod is worthwhile. Most unscrew into three pieces, which can be handy. Two sections are more convenient when cleaning shorter, slug barrels.

Break-free solvent, which covers just about everything.

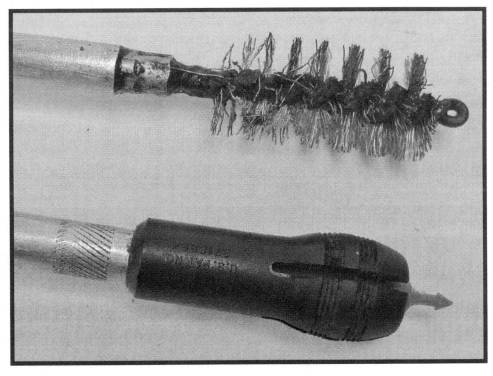

Shotgun rods and handy tips for brushing or swabbing barrel.

Protective gear. Hearing and eye protection are a must. You can spend extra money on electronic muffs, but a basic set will do. Ear plugs offer less protection. With younger shooters, doubling up with plugs and muffs can help protect delicate hearing.

Shooting essentials: don't skip hearing and eye protection!

HANDGUNS

You can probably use the same protective gear and cleaning kit, but you'll need some important extras. One key item is a quality holster.

Holster. Without full attention, it's very easy to endanger others by allowing your muzzle to wander around. During any handgun events other than a firing range booth or stall, a holster is the safest means to maintain muzzle discipline. Unfortunately, an improper choice may be equally unsafe. We don't like designs requiring both hands to re-holster because the support hand invariably will be swept by a muzzle. Shoulder rigs can cause the same problem, and horizontal-carry models violate Rule #2. Stand behind someone wearing one and you'll be looking down their barrel. Some sort of retention device is advisable, as is a secure attachment system. Believe it or not, a proper, stiff belt is equally important.

An all-important holster, shown with matching magazine pouch.

<u>Magazines or loader-devices.</u> If you've chosen a pistol, you'll need spare magazines. A total of three represent a good starting point. Revolver shooters should learn how to use an appropriately named speedloader, of which two are recommended.

Revolver speed-loader designs: S&W Model 625 N-frame, .45 ACP with moon-clips (T), 686 L-frame, .357 with Safariland competition loaders.

Range bag. You'll need a way to safely lug your handgun, magazines, and ammo. Some targets would be helpful, with a means to put them up. A stapler and other items will soon fill the bag, so buy one large enough for future growth. A few boxes of ammo create extra weight, so rugged construction and a sturdy shoulder strap are recommended.

122

Don't forget a range bag to carry all your goodies.
Your glasses and muffs should be permanent passengers.

Handgun vault. Depending on your personal situation, you may (or may not) need an alternate and secure handgun storage option capable of emergency access. The portable lockboxes detailed in the gun safe chapter are a good choice. They're quicker to access than a full-blown safe and are fairly affordable. Firearms and ammunition should really be stored separately, so placing a loaded handgun in your main safe is not advisable. Using a pistol equipped with a magazine disconnect, one can just pop the mag and lock it in the box. It's not perfect, but it is a whole lot better than nothing.

OTHER GEAR

So far, we've been dealing with accessories related to individual systems. However, we're not out of the woods quite yet. Some other equipment will need to be on hand. A few that come to mind are a bipod, sandbag rest, laser rangefinder, a tactical light, knife, and serviceable binoculars.

A sand-bag rest is essential for any serious accuracy testing.

"More goodies: note the QD Safariland RLS light mounted above the Harris Bipod."

Don't expect to buy a useful set of binos for $75. You won't need to spend $1,000 (or more) for a top-shelf set, but you'd better budget a few hundred bucks for a decent pair. Anything less is just money wasted. You might be surprised at how well a set of quality binoculars works after dark. We routinely use them in conjunction with specialized night vision instruments for nocturnal surveillance. Granted, they won't perform to the same level, but they can reveal objects of interest. Batteries aren't a concern and our own night vision is preserved. Of all the gear listed so far, binoculars are near the top.

Bushnell's general-purpose 10x42 Legends are an affordable choice.
The ultra-compact 7x20 Leupolds sacrifice performance for size.

SUMMARY

As you can see, the cost of each firearm is really just a starting point. True "system cost" will be much higher, and should be figured into the budget. In other words, you can burn through a large stack of cash. Without the right information, it's easy to waste your money on useless or unsafe gear.

Chapter 12: The Follow-up Manuals

If you purchase a gun safe and attempt to fill it up in one fell swoop, you'll be hemorrhaging dollar bills. To keep things manageable, why not adopt an incremental approach? That's exactly what's been done with the succession of firearms manuals. You can focus on just one system and chip away until the essentials have been procured. The old saying, "a little knowledge is a dangerous thing" certainly holds true with firearms. Accordingly, each subsequent manual in this series serves as a source for in-depth knowledge pertinent to specific systems. Furthermore, each is geared toward survival-based roles and the core principles espoused in this book.

THE MANUALS

The PrepSmart Shotgun Manual: Would you like a bird gun, riot gun, and high powered rifle all rolled into one single shotgun? Where's the tradeoff on recoil and performance? What shells work best with different chokes? This manual covers everything you ever wanted to know about shotguns. Technical aspects are explored including the different types of guns, gauges, shells, chokes, shot sizes, and ballistics. Accessories are examined, along with training tips and other useful information. The human factor is addressed with methods to accommodate smaller-statured shooters. Putting it all together, you'll not only have serious defensive capabilities, but also a means for the harvesting of both small and very large game. The *Shotgun Manual* will show you the way.

The PrepSmart Rimfire & Airgun Manual: Did you know you can set up a .22 rimfire or airgun as a scaled down long range trainer? You can with the right rifle and scope. How about special .22 ammo or an airgun as quiet a silencer? Which types of rifles are best for your needs? This publication covers everything you'll need to know about rimfire rifles and airguns. The different types are examined, along with various calibers and their limitations. A wide range of ammunition and power plants are explored, including some very unusual choices. Scopes and other sighting systems are detailed, as are useful accessories. Junior shooters aren't ignored, and you'll find tips for more experienced shooters as well. Practice regimens are outlined to help develop transferable big bore skills. The *Rimfire & Airgun Manual* is your source for small bore technologies, from training through hunting. It's also a stepping stone to the next publication.

The PrepSmart Centerfire Rifle & AR-15 Manual: Are you interested in lever guns or semi-auto rifles? How about bolt actions; or an entire family of guns in different calibers? How do you choose the right scope, and how do you sight it in? How do you select the most accurate loads, or pick the right bullets? How do you reduce recoil for younger shooters? Following in the steps of the Rimfire & Airgun Manual, the centerfire book takes you to the next level. Optics and ballistic aiming systems are explored, along with skill building regimens. You'll see methods to assess true accuracy, and other useful tips. Different calibers and loads are discussed, as are various rifle choices. The AR-15 has grown wildly popular, with dozens of brands and hundreds of accessories to choose from. It's an extremely versatile platform for good reason, and can be instantly transformed to many different profiles. Switch top conversions are possible in .22 LR through several pistol calibers, and serious big bore rounds. On top of that, universal "Picatinny" mounting points will easily accommodate nearly unlimited optical or equipment choices. Since most of us don't have unlimited funds, we'll determine exactly *which* accessories are necessary. This edition is the next progression in our system-based approach for development of a practical firearms battery.

The PrepSmart Handgun Manual: You can shoot yourself with the wrong combination of pistol, holster, and clothing, so which ones are dangerous? You may understand the fundamentals of shooting, but how do they apply to handguns? Are you interested in a 1911 pistol? If so, did you know you can create your own multi-caliber pistol off a single frame? What about other types? Which loads are your best defensive choices? This publication covers everything you'll need to know about handguns, from different models through practical calibers, holsters, and accessories. You'll see some interesting alternatives to six shot revolvers, and the latest high capacity pistols. The smaller guns are covered, too. Practical revolver and pistol skills are detailed, along with recommended practice regimens. The *Handgun Manual* rolls all of this information into one source for safe and effective handling.

If you have enjoyed this manual, we kindly ask that you tell a friend or write a review on Amazon, Facebook, or other channels. Thank you for your support.

www.PrepperPress.com/PrepSmart

44735960R00076

Made in the USA
Lexington, KY
07 September 2015